He Hears

Your

Prayers

He Hears Your Prayers

Simple Steps to God

- Ron Auch -

New Leaf Press

Dedication

This book is dedicated to all those who long for a more intimate relationship with our Lord. And to those who, over the years, have continually encouraged me to keep teaching the principles of prayer found in this book.

Acknowledgment

I am once again compelled to acknowledge the incalculable help of John Cronce. This is the seventh book he has edited for me. He is truly a most vital part of this ministry team.

Table of Contents

Introduction

And I will give them an heart to know me, that I am the Lord: and they shall be my people, and I will be their God: for they shall return unto me with their whole heart (Jer. 24:7).

He Hears Your Prayers will take us on a wonderful adventure into intimacy with God. It is not enough to simply know about God; we must know Him. <u>Prayer is the only means to knowing God.</u> In this book we will examine what it is to draw close to the Lord and develop an intimate relationship with Him.

We will be looking at a number of different aspects of prayer as well as the practices, or how-to's, of spending time in prayer. However, the primary focus of this book will be developing a lifestyle of seeking God.

Developing a heart that seeks God comes through our personal prayer life, which differs from what we call public prayer or a group prayer meeting. I believe in group prayer meetings, but I also believe that the group prayer meeting is void of power today because of the lack of private prayer.

Charles Finney, one of the great revivalists of the past, once said, "Short public prayer is only made powerful through long private prayer." Finney once conducted a revival in Rome, New York, where eventually every person in the city surrendered his or her life to Christ. Finney often commented on how he would walk down the street in the middle of the day and could hear people praying and crying out to God in their homes for the evening meeting. That sort of thing is a missing element in the believer's life today.

We tend to put all our hopes on the gathering (church service). We hope that when we get there everything will happen, and that we'll be fully revived. It's not that that's not possible, it's just that we often fail to do what we could do to make the gathering much more powerful than it is, hence, private prayer. Seeking God personally, in the prayer closet, is what this book is about.

Chapter One

The Necessity of Prayer

e are going to begin by looking at the necessity of prayer and four of the things that it leads to. This is not meant to be an exhaustive list, for certainly prayer leads to many things. This is to simply give us a greater understanding of how necessary prayer really is.

1. Prayer leads to salvation.

> If thou <u>shalt confess</u> with thy *Confess*
> mouth the Lord Jesus, and <u>shalt believe</u> *believe*
> in thine heart that God hath raised him   *=*
> from the dead, <u>thou shalt be saved.</u> For *Salvation*
> with the <u>heart</u> man <u>believeth</u> unto righ-
> teousness; and with the <u>mouth</u> <u>confes-</u>
> <u>sion</u> is made unto salvation (Rom.
> 10:9-10).

heart believes + mouth Confesses.

These verses show us how important prayer is. We don't earn our salvation by praying enough, but rather, it teaches that we are saved by asking Christ into our lives and by confessing Him as Lord.

Confession is prayer. If prayer never accomplished anything other than this one single thing (salvation), it would make it the most important thing we could do. We enter into our relationship with Christ through prayer.

Not only does prayer establish our relationship with Christ, it goes on to enhance that relationship. It is needed not only to begin, but also to nurture the relationship.

2. The second thing prayer leads to is divine fellowship.

> Behold, I stand at the door, *of your heart* and knock: if any man hear my voice, and open the door, I will come in to him, and will sup with him, and he with me (Rev. 3:20).

The act of supping (eating) is that of divine fellowship. There is no fellowship with God outside of prayer. Some take exception to that and say, "We have an ever-abiding presence of the Holy Spirit in us all the time, and therefore, we don't need to specifically set aside time for prayer — our life is a prayer."

We do have an ever-abiding presence of the Lord in us, but to fellowship with Him, we need to specifically set aside time just for Him. Being a Christian doesn't mean that we automatically fellowship with other Christians. In order to fellowship with other Christians, we have to be with them.

Have we ever considered why Jesus prayed so much? This used to concern me because I thought, *If anybody had God figured out, Jesus did, so why did He need to pray so much?* One day the Lord just spoke to my heart and said, "Jesus did not pray to figure Me out. Jesus prayed because He had Me figured out."

In other words, Jesus prayed out of the respect He had for His Father. It's because of what Jesus knew about God that He honored Him with His time. Jesus knew it would be disrespectful not to pray. Jesus wanted to sup with His Father. Therefore, He prayed alone often. "And he withdrew himself into the wilderness, and prayed" (Luke 5:16).

3. The third item is spiritual growth.

In Acts 6:4 we read, "But we will give ourselves continually to prayer, and to the ministry of the word." The Early Church was rapidly growing. The Apostles were being weighed down with a multitude of responsibilities. Some of their responsibilities were taking them away from their spiritual growth. So they appointed deacons to help them with those responsibilities. As spiritual leaders they realized they needed to continue to grow spiritually. They determined they would do that by giving themselves continually to prayer and the ministry of the Word.

This is a book about prayer, so obviously we are going to focus on that subject. However, I do not intend to minimize the importance of the Word of God. The early Christian leaders gave themselves to prayer and the ministry of the Word. They recognized that they needed to have both elements in their lives, just like we have to have both.

Every point we will be making in this study uses a Bible verse as its reference. Far from leaving out the Bible, I am simply telling you what the Bible says about prayer.

Prayer operates in a spiritual realm, whereas the Word of God is very down-to-earth. If we don't have both prayer and the Word in our lives, we are out of balance. If all we do is prayer and no Word, we tend to get so heavenly minded that we are no earthly good. If all we have is the Word and no prayer, we tend to get legalistic. We have to have both in order to be balanced. We can take either thing to an extreme.

The Pharisees could not be accused of not knowing the Word, and yet Jesus was not impressed with their knowledge of God's Word at all because they lacked spiritual insight. They had no intimacy with God. They also had prayer in their lives, but they had not surrendered their hearts to God. Subsequently, they did not impress Jesus at all.

This book is not about getting us to pray more. It's about getting us to want God more. The lack of prayer comes from the lack of desire for God. We cannot have deep desires for God and continue to ignore His presence. Anyone we desire, we long to be with. If we are relatively prayer-less it's because we lack a hunger for God. We are to hunger and thirst for righteousness; then we shall be filled.

If it were a matter of simply praying a lot, we would be nothing more than the Pharisees. They prayed a lot but had no relationship. When a person's prayer life comes out of his desire to be with God, then he develops intimacy with God and his praying is not just a religious activity.

"Jesus answered and said unto them, Ye do err, not knowing the scriptures, nor the power of God" (Matt. 22:29). Jesus was telling His disciples that their problem was that they did not have a good knowledge of either the Word or the power (prayer). We must have a love for both God's Word and God's presence if we are to become well-balanced Christians.

4. Unexplained miracles also prove the necessity of prayer.

In Acts 12:5 we read, "Peter therefore was kept in prison: but prayer was made without ceasing of the church unto God for him." In this account, when Peter was put in jail unjustly, the church went to prayer, unto God, without ceasing, for Peter. After the church prayed, Peter's chains fell off miraculously and the prison doors opened up.

> And, behold, the angel of the Lord came upon him, and a light shined in the prison: and he smote Peter on the side, and raised him up, saying, Arise up quickly. And his chains fell off from his hands (Acts 12:7).

What do we think that this church was praying for Peter? If we had an unjustly imprisoned friend, what would we pray for him? I believe that they were praying for his release. Suddenly an angel appeared, he was miraculously freed from prison, and then went to the house where they were praying and knocked on the door. After Rhoda answered the door and asked who it was, he said, "It's me, Peter."

> And when she knew Peter's voice, she opened not the gate for gladness, but ran in, and told how Peter stood before the gate. And they said unto her, Thou art mad. But she constantly affirmed that it was even so. Then said they, It is his angel. But Peter continued knocking: and when they had opened the door, and saw him, they were astonished (Acts 12:14-16).

When Rhoda told them that Peter was at the door, their response was, in essence, "He can't be, he's in jail, and we're praying that God will free him. How can Peter be here? That would be an answer to prayer." This is an account of an unexplained miracle, in the sense that God actually answered their prayer even in their unbelief.

God takes us where we are, and works with us from that point. He cannot wait until we achieve a certain level, and then begin to work with us. He has to help us achieve any level of faith. Therefore, He works with us from where we are in order to move us to the next level of faith. It's sort of like the man who said with tears, "Lord, I believe; help thou mine unbelief" (Mark 9:24).

If the church that prayed for Peter were to pray a second time for someone in jail, their faith level would be much higher. Then, when there was a knock on the door, they wouldn't be surprised. They would probably have said, "We expected this to happen. It happened before and we just knew it would happen again."

They would have had an entirely different reaction because their faith would have grown through their experience.

One of the most important things we can do is pray. We must talk to our Creator to learn more about ourselves and more about Him.

Chapter Two

The Nature of Prayer

e come now to the nature of prayer. In this chapter we will look at some of the intrinsic characteristics and qualities of prayer. It is important to understand the inherent facets of seeking God. If we are to become people who know their God, and who communicate with their God, then we must be able to comprehend the essence of this subject.

Talking to God

The most basic attribute of prayer is talking to God. Hosea 14:2 says, "Take with you words, and turn to the Lord."

Talk to God! It's really not that difficult, but that does not mean prayer is a simplistic thing either. When my family came to the Lord, we had a Bible study in our home. We invited an elder from our church to do the teaching. During one of our studies, he taught about prayer. The question was asked, "What is prayer?"

"Well," he said, "It's talking to God."

"How do you talk to God?" someone asked.

"You talk to God the same that you would talk to anybody," he responded.

I came to realize later that the problem most people have is not that of talking, but rather, that of knowing. We can talk to any person, but unless we really know a person, our talk is very superficial. The same is true with God. Prayer is talking to God, but until we get to know God, our conversation will be sort of shallow.

We typically begin our prayer lives asking God for things because we are young, we are babes in Christ. However, the more time we spend with God, the more we get to know God, and then the nature of our conversation changes. The depth of it changes. As we get to know God we begin to realize that He is honestly interested in our lives. In time, we begin to allow God to handle the complexities of our lives.

Therefore, talking is not the problem, as much as knowing is. The only way to get to know the Father is through prayer. The more we get to know God, the more natural the conversation is. We may feel that we are not very eloquent pray-ers initially, but that will change with time. Everything becomes more natural with practice.

Focusing God's Power

In Exodus 9:33 we read:

> And Moses went out of the city
> from Pharaoh, and spread abroad his

hands unto the Lord: and the thunders
and hail ceased, and the rain was not
poured upon the earth.

In this account, Moses was trying to free the Hebrew children from Pharaoh's grip, but he would not
let them go. Moses went out of the city, spread abroad
his hands and prayed. Moses "prayed in" a drought.
He directed the power of God unto his specific circumstances.

One of the unique things about prayer is that it
can be all-encompassing, and it can be very specific.
We can pray for the whole world if we choose. God
has a great satellite system. We can send a prayer to
God, and He can project it to any place on the earth.
Psalm 2:8 reads: "Ask of me, and I shall give thee
the heathen for thine inheritance, and the uttermost
parts of the earth for thy possession." A person can
pray from wherever they are and can touch any part
of the earth, even the uttermost parts of the earth.

We can pray for the whole world, but we can also
pray for a very specific need or situation. The same
power of God that parted the Red Sea and caused all
of the miracles we read about in the Old Testament,
can be brought to our own homes. We can focus the
power of God on our own communities through prayer.

Hearing God

Hearing God is one of the more puzzling aspects
of prayer. Some people claim to hear God all the time,

while others seem to rarely hear Him. When people refer to "hearing God," it seems each person has had a different experience.

> God, who at sundry times and in divers manners spake in time past unto the fathers by the prophets, Hath in these last days spoken unto us by his Son, whom he hath appointed heir of all things, by whom also he made the worlds (Heb. 1:1-2).

The writer of Hebrews said that God spoke in many different ways and in many different times. However, today, He speaks to us through His Son.

I believe very much in God's ability to speak to us in whatever way He may choose, but the Scripture indicates that He wants to communicate to us primarily through a relationship with His Son. There is more to hearing God than simply becoming "good" at understanding what God is saying. God wants to communicate with His children, but without a proper relationship with Him, He would simply be passing messages on to us.

Isaiah 30:18 will give us more insight into this issue:

> And therefore will the Lord wait, that he may be gracious unto you, and therefore will he be exalted, that he may have mercy upon you: for the Lord is a

> God of judgment: <u>blessed are all they</u>
> <u>that wait for him,</u>

"Blessed are all they that wait for Him." There are times when God will wait, to teach us to wait. A closer rendering to the <u>original language reveals that</u> <u>this verse is actually saying that God wants to an-</u> <u>swer our prayer, that He even longs to be gracious to</u> <u>us, but that He will wait. We may ask, "Why is it that</u> <u>God would wait if He actually longs to answer our</u> <u>prayer?"</u> The answer to that comes from what I call the "greater good." God responds according to the "greater good."

God wants to bring each of us to a place of trust as stated in Proverbs 3:5, <u>"Trust in the Lord with all</u> <u>thine heart; and lean not unto thine own understand-</u> <u>ing."</u> We are going to have to come to the place of honestly believing that God knows things we don't understand.

I will give you an example of this. My son, for the first time in his life, was able to ride a motorcycle, at my brother's house. My brother lives on a farm, and his son owns a motorcycle designed for children. After his ride, my son came back fully convinced that he should have his own motorcycle. As a dad, I can relate to his desire and would actually like for him to have one. However, he was only eight years old at the time. We live in the city, and it's against the law for children to even ride them there. There are a number of things that I understand about the situation, that my son does not understand. In a certain sense I can identify with how God longs to be gracious but cannot actually answer our prayer at the moment.

If I would have granted my son his request, it would have proven to be the wrong thing to do. I come from a perspective that he cannot have. My perspective comes from my experience and maturity. There is no possible way for my son to understand things the way I see them. I can sit down with my son and explain to him how I would like him to have a motorcycle someday but that it would not be the right thing to do now. Even if I make perfect sense, he will not accept it. He will have a counter-reaction for each one of my reasons.

Children believe they understand, but there is no way they can. We are nothing more than children of God. Many times we pray for things that God would actually like to answer, but when He says, "Wait," we have a fit. We believe we can see the picture perfectly, when in reality, we cannot see from God's perspective. There is no way for us to have God's perspective. We think we understand but we don't.

Suppose that when I told my son that he would have to wait and trust what I said, his reaction was, "Okay Dad, based on what you know rather than what I know, I will be glad to wait!" How do you believe I would react as a father? First, I would probably faint. After recovering, I would say to him, "Blessed are you my son for waiting." That is why Isaiah 30:18 ends by saying, "Blessed are all they that wait for Him."

Then in verse 21 of Isaiah 30 it says: "And thine

ears shall hear a word behind thee, saying, This is the way, walk ye in it, when ye turn to the right hand, and when ye turn to the left." This verse is telling us that if we learn how to wait on the Lord, we will get to a place where we understand (hear) what He's saying. When we walk the way He asks us to walk, we exalt Him because we walk in His path.

To understand verse 21 more fully, we must go back and look deeper into the word "wait." In the Hebrew language, it deals with someone who has braided himself to God. It's like having both hands so gripped onto God, that if God moves, you move, or if God waits, you wait. In Isaiah 40:31 we see an excellent use of this word: "But they that wait upon the Lord shall renew their strength; they shall mount up with wings as eagles; they shall run, and not be weary; and they shall walk, and not faint." The word "wait" has more to do with attaching ourselves to something than it has to do with actually sitting around waiting. It's actually attaching ourselves to the Lord. This has to do with relationship. Attaching yourself to someone is that of developing a relationship with him.

When I was a little boy, every time I had some money I would go down to the store at the end of our street to spend it. When the kids in my neighborhood and I would walk into that store, we would see many different things, but the first thing we would see was a big candy counter full of chocolate; next to that was a fresh fruit counter. We had many different ways to spend that money. My mom was always trying to get me to eat the right foods. As I would stand there trying to figure out how to spend my money, my mom would speak to me. My mom was not actually in the store. She didn't even have to be there. I simply knew her so well, that even though she was not there, suddenly I would hear a word behind me saying, "Ron, this is the way, walk ye in it!" This is the same type of thing Isaiah is saying. If we knew Jesus to the same degree that we know our own parents, we will find that when we have decisions to make, our directions will be based what we understand about Him. My decision on how to spend the money was based on who I knew my mom to be. It's almost as though I could hear her voice audibly. Even though I didn't actually hear her voice, she spoke to me through her personality. If we learn to wait on God, or attach ourselves to God, we will develop a relationship with Him that speaks to us constantly. Our hearing will be based on who we know Jesus to be. Prayer plays an important part here. The only way for a relationship to develop is through spending time in someone's presence. If we are to develop a relationship with Christ, we must spend time with Him.

Gaining Direction

I hear God because I have been praying about something, rather than hearing Him while I'm in prayer. Some people seem to hear God speak to them while they are in prayer. I am not one of those type of people. My prayer time is not like a two-way conver-

sation where I sit down with God and talk to Him
and then He talks back to me. However, I may find
myself driving down the road and see something or
hear something and then realize that God is speaking
to me about the thing I have been in prayer about.

Many times we will hear people refer to God
speaking to them and we draw the conclusion that
they sat down and talked freely to God. Ministers
will do this quite often. They may be teaching and
say, "God told me exactly what I needed to hear."
Usually what they are referring to is the end result of
a long process. They don't necessarily fill us in on
how long it took to get their answer, they simply refer to the answer and actually can create (without re-
alizing it) a false impression about hearing God.

Nothing will sharpen our ability to hear God like
spending time in His presence. There is simply no
substitute. We try to sharpen our spiritual hearing
through certain steps of faith or spiritual exercises
when in reality, if we want to know someone's voice,
all we need to do is spend time with him.

Ministering to the Lord

We now want to consider ministering to the Lord.
Psalms 95:2 says, "Let us come before his presence
with thanksgiving; Let us shout joyfully to Him with
psalms." This brings us to worship. Worship should
be on the cutting edge of your prayer life. If worship
is done properly, it is very much prayer. Worship is
prayer. Sometimes when I tell people that they should

develop a lifestyle of spending a minimum of an hour in prayer a day, many of them say, "I don't have that many requests for God. They would never fill a whole hour every day."

Typically we have narrow vision, especially concerning prayer. Certainly petition is a part of the prayer life, but it is only a part. Worship is also prayer. Worship is probably one of the more pleasurable parts of prayer. Most of the rest of the prayer life consists of getting something from God, but in worship we get to minister to the Lord. Most of prayer is God ministering to us, but in worship we minister to Him; that makes it unique and precious. It is one of the few things we are able to do to purposely bless Him.

It is important to begin our prayer time worshipping God. Worship centralizes God and decentralizes self. It gets our minds off of ourselves and on to our God. In my worship time I will sing songs to the Lord, I will tell Him how much I love Him and want Him. I will express His greatness and my dependency upon Him. I worship Him! After I have spent sufficient time in worship, I will enter into the other facets of prayer.

Chapter Three

The Neglect of Prayer

id you know that it is not "spiritually" natural to neglect prayer? When the Spirit of God dwells in us, He draws us into the presence of God. However, if prayer is disregarded long enough, we can dull His spiritual sensitivity.

Jeremiah 2:32 says, "Can a virgin forget her ornaments, Or a bride her attire? Yet my people have forgotten Me days without number." The prophet tells us that it is as natural to spend time in prayer as it is for a bride to remember her wedding garment. Then he makes a statement that reveals the spiritual depravity of God's people: "Yet my people have forgotten me days without number." To be able to go day after day without setting specific time aside to be with God would be like a bride planning her wedding but continually forgetting to concern herself with what she will wear during the ceremony.

It is not hard to go through a whole day without giving any time to seeking God unless we purposely set aside time for prayer. However, the people of God, in Jeremiah's day, had gone so many days without spending any time with God that the amount of days could not be numbered. When was the last time we set aside some time just to be in the presence of God? I am not talking about praying for meals, or even while we are in a meeting. What we are dealing with here is about deliberately setting aside time just to pray.

The Average Prayer Life

It is not uncommon to find people today who really have no prayer life outside of Church. The majority of Christians today only pray at the end of a church service. The typical time around the altar is about 5 minutes. Suppose a person's church was experiencing a revival to the point that everybody was praying 30 minutes after the service. The sum total of their prayer life would be 30 minutes a week. That would exceed the national average by six times. Thirty minutes a week multiplied by four weeks would come out to 2 hours a month in prayer. Two hours a month multiplied by 12 months would come out to 24 hours (one day) a year in prayer.

Many people have worked deep-seated problems into their lives. Some of these problems have developed over many years. If we have deep problems and give God the equivalent of one day worth of prayer out of 365 days, we don't deserve to ask God, "Why haven't you changed me?" How many of us are praying today for the same spiritual problems we prayed about a year ago? Our lack of time in prayer is causing us to simply spin our wheels. We are not really progressing spiritually. If we compare someone who has a prayer life (someone who prays 1 hour a day, or 365 hours a year in prayer) to someone who only prays at church (24 hours of prayer a year) we have a difference of 341 hours a year in the presence of God.

Spiritual progression is nothing more than developing in Christ's likeness. If we are growing spiritually, it's because we are becoming more and more like Christ. The only way to become like Christ is to be with Him. Spending time in His presence is the only way to become like Him. The Book of Proverbs teaches us that the way to become angry is to spend time with an angry man; if you want to become wise, spend time with a wise man. Parents face this dilemma all the time. It is not uncommon for a parent to say to their children, "If you run around with that group of kids, you are going to start looking like them." The spirit of the individuals we spend time with begins to develop in us. If we want to become like Christ, spend time with Him. It is a simple thing to become religious. It is quite another thing to become like Christ.

Self-Centered

When we neglect prayer, it indicates three things about ourselves. The first thing is that we are self-centered. Psalms 10:4 states: "The wicked, through the pride of his countenance, will not seek after God: God is not in all his thoughts." Pride, or self, is our biggest deterrent to prayer. Our lives tend to center around the big "I." Subsequently, we really don't have time for anything else. All of our prayer excuses begin with "I." "I don't have time," or "I'm too tired," are common excuses for not praying. Prayer is God-centered. Therefore, everything less than prayer is self-centered.

Have we ever considered what the original sin actually is? We often refer to Eve eating the fruit as the original sin. It actually happened prior to that. The original sin took place in Heaven. When Lucifer became proud and wanted to be as God, he committed the original sin. "For God doth know that in the day ye eat thereof, then your eyes shall be opened, and ye shall be as gods, knowing good and evil" (Gen. 3:5). When the serpent deceived Eve, he did it by appealing to her pride.

Satan is the master of pride. It was because of pride that he lost his position in heaven. He approached Eve and said in essence, "Wouldn't you like to be like God?" Satan told her that if she ate the fruit, she would be as a god, knowing good and evil. From that day on, man has sought to be as God. Wanting to be as God is an exaltation of oneself.

Prayer is an act of humility. When we bow our knees and come face to face with the one true God, we are continually reminded of who we really are. That's humbling! God is not even in the thoughts of wicked men, because of their pride. The nature of wickedness is self-centeredness. If a person is truly self-centered, he will find it very difficult to give himself over to a life of prayer.

Slothful

Jeremiah 48:10 says, "Cursed be he that doeth the work of the Lord deceitfully (slothful)." The word "deceitful" is translated "slothful." To be slothful in regards to the work of God is to be indifferent concerning its effectiveness. It's to attempt to do it without prayer. It is not difficult for the "work of God" to replace the "God of the work." When we are busy about the work of God, we feel justified in not having spent any time in prayer because, after all, we are working for God. However, we really cannot do the "work of God" without the blessing of the "God of the work." If we are slothful, we lack God's blessing. In fact, we are cursed.

I had a personal friend who determined that he was going to be the pastor of a large church. When he first became a pastor, his church was small, so he gave himself to doing everything there was to do. He did the preaching, the teaching, the cleaning, the visiting, the repair work — he did it all. Not long after he started, he had a heart attack. As he was lying on the recovery table he began to pray, "Lord, you need to heal me, so I can get back to the church."

The Lord answered him by asking, "Why do I need to get you back to your church so soon?"

After some thought the pastor responded, "Because it will die without me."

Once the pastor realized that he was doing everything and wasn't really depending upon God, the Lord spoke something to him that changed his life.

God said, "The Lord of the work is always more important than the work of the Lord!"

God was calling him to prayer. He wanted that pastor to be a man who sought God. My friend determined from that day on to be a man of prayer and let God do His work. He went on to build the largest church in his region, but he did it through prayer. Once he put the God of the work before the work of God, everything began to work the way it should.

Don't be slothful, be prayerful. Consider God's instruction to the church in Ephesus:

> I know thy works, and thy labour, and thy patience, and how thou canst not bear them which are evil: and thou hast tried them which say they are apostles, and are not, and hast found them liars: And hast borne, and hast patience, and for my name's sake hast laboured, and hast not fainted. Nevertheless I have somewhat against thee, because thou hast left thy first love (Rev. 2:2-4).

Ephesus had a church that was very busy concerning the work of the Lord. They worked hard, they had patience, they did not tolerate evil, they knew how to test the Apostles, and they never gave up. However, in the midst of this glowing report God says, "Nevertheless I have something against you, you have forsaken your first love."

A believer with first love desires is completely taken up with Jesus himself. It's being infatuated with Him. It's wanting Him. It's longing for His presence, but it's also humbling. In order to gain more of Christ, we have to have less and less of ourselves. If a person wants Christ, he can no longer have himself; he can no longer put himself first in his life.

If a person is content with the lack of self-exaltation, then he can remain in his first love status. However, if a person wants some recognition, he looks for ways to accomplish that. It is not uncommon to find believers seeking exaltation through the status they have in "the work of God." Subsequently, their whole focus becomes the work of God. We can gain great status through our positions in God's work. However, we are to only concern ourselves with the exaltation of Christ, not ourselves.

Ephesus was not accused of being lazy. She was accused of being slothful. Slothfulness relates to our spiritual pursuit of God, not our service for God.

Sinfulness

Did you know that it is a sin not to pray? First Samuel 12:23 states: "Moreover as for me, God forbid that I should sin against the Lord in ceasing to pray for you." How does the lack of prayer become a sin? To answer that, it will be important to understand the two different types of sin there are. There are sins of commission and sins of omission. A sin of commission is an outward sin. It's an overt action. It's like having full knowledge that what you are about to do is wrong, but doing it anyway. It's like driving your car and seeing a stop sign and saying, "By an act of my will, I will run this stop sign." A sin of commission is that of doing the evil that we know we should not do.

There is also the sin of omission. Sins of omission are not as outwardly obvious but they are just as sinful. The story of the good Samaritan reveals this. In this story a man had been beaten and robbed and was lying on the road in need of help. A priest came walking by but instead of helping him, he went around him. When he walked around the man he committed a sin of omission.

A sin of omission is described in James 4:17: "Therefore to him that knoweth to do good, and doeth it not, to him it is sin." Sins of omission differ from sins of commission. Sins of commission fall under the category of doing the evil we should not do. Sins of omission fall under the category of refusing to do the good we know we should do.

Omission doesn't look as bad because it's not as obvious. It's simply that of not doing what we should do. That's the category prayerlessness falls under. If we are not people of prayer then we are not doing the good we know we could be doing. To understand the power of prayer but fail to develop our prayer life is to know to do good but not do it.

Chapter Four

The Results of Prayer

here are many things the Bible tells us that we can expect as a result of prayer. Many people have wonderful testimonies of how the Lord has answered prayer. Many of the testimonies we hear have to do with the Lord blessing us materially. However, there is another aspect of praying that we must consider, also. We rarely look into what prayer prevents. We primarily look into what prayer causes rather than in what praying has done to prevent serious consequences from happening.

Prayer prevents much more than it causes. The problem with this aspect of prayer is that it is not as visible as answered prayer is. Subsequently, we don't focus on it very much. We can measure answered prayers. Some people carry a prayer journal in which they list all of their requests and then in a column beside the request, they list the answers as they come. A person can look back at that and see something tangible. However, that which prayer prevents cannot be listed this way. We have no way of knowing how the prayers of our parents kept us from disaster when we were young. There is no way of knowing how the prayers of a mate have kept their spouse from temptation.

In Hebrews 7:25 we read: "Wherefore he is able also to save them to the uttermost that come unto God by him, seeing he ever liveth to make intercession for them." Jesus ever lives to intercede for us. How many times have we avoided tragedy because of the prayers of our Saviour?

Wisdom

Wisdom is a result of prayer that averts many disasters. When our lives are directed by the wisdom that God gives, we make the decisions He would have us make. Obviously that would be the safest way for any person to live.

James 1:5 tell us: "If any of you lack wisdom, let him ask of God, that giveth to all men liberally, and upbraideth not; and it shall be given him." I used to pray for wisdom and then when I was finished praying, I would sit back and try to figure out if I was any smarter. I came to realize later that there is a difference between wisdom and intelligence. We can be very intelligent fools and we can be very wise common men, because wisdom and intellect are two different things. I was basically praying for intelligence, thinking I was asking God for wisdom.

In the Book of Proverbs, wisdom is always connected with obedience. It basically says that wisdom is all the knowledge and understanding necessary for a consistent Christian walk. Consistency in our walk with God is the pinnacle of wisdom. We could not give an example of a man who is wiser than a man totally obedient to God. That is the pinnacle of wisdom. How could anyone exceed obedience to God? If we obey God in all things, it's because we are wise. The lack of obedience shows our foolishness. If we make a conscious effort to pray more, then we are making an indirect decision to be more obedient to the Lord. We cannot continue to draw close to God and remain disobedient to Him. The desire to draw close to God allows God a freedom to work on all the disobedience in our lives. We cannot get close to God while there is disobedience to Him, because disobedience is what keeps us from closeness to Him.

If we say, "Lord, I'm going to pray more. I'm going to give myself over to prayer because I want to be close to you," God then goes to work to remove the things that keep us from closeness to Him.

We have an option; we can either allow God to work in us, or we will stop working with God. We have the prerogative that when God starts dealing with something that we don't want Him to deal with, we can just stop praying. I do not recommend doing that. However, God doesn't take away our free will, nor does prayer. We can still choose to sin if we want to sin. However, if we really have a heart for God and want to draw closer and closer to Him, then we will choose not to sin, for that would hinder our closeness with Him.

Acts 9:5 teaches us something very important. "And he said, Who art thou, Lord? And the Lord said, I am Jesus whom thou persecutest: it is hard for thee to kick against the pricks." In this account Paul is on the road to Damascus when he has a divine encounter with Jesus himself. Paul inquires about who it is he is meeting. Jesus identifies himself and then says, "It is hard for thee to kick against the pricks." The Greek meaning for the word "pricks" is "divine impulse." In other words, God had apparently been working in Paul's life for some time at this point, and He says, in essence, you cannot continue to kick against the work (divine impulses) of the Holy Spirit. The Holy Spirit gets under our skin and continually prods us until we reform. We will either give in to Him and reform, or we will stop doing that which causes Him to get under our skin, i.e., praying.

If we are praying to become more obedient to the Lord, we quickly begin to see that through obedience we take on the mind of Christ. We do things the way God does things, and that results in wisdom, which is the ability to remain consistent in our walk with God.

Deliverance

Prayer also results in deliverance. Psalms 34:4 says, "I sought the Lord, and he heard me, and delivered me from all my fears." David said that he sought the Lord, and that is what delivered him from his fears.

When I was a little boy, my parents took me to a

swimming pool to teach me how to swim. I was probably only about four years old, and I remember my
mom walking me down to one end of the pool and
saying, "Jump in."

I didn't want to just jump in.

She said, "You can just jump in, this isn't over
your head." I didn't want to simply jump in, so finally my dad got in the water, held out his arms and
said, "Jump in and I'll catch you." Then I could for
two reasons; one is that I knew my dad loved me,
and the other is that I knew my dad was strong. When
I combined his love with his strength, I realized I
could jump into a situation where, under different circumstances, I would have been frightened. Knowing
my dad is what delivered me from my fears.

The Psalmist said, "I sought the Lord." David
got to know God, and that is what delivered him
from his fear. Learning who God is, delivers us. The
New Testament puts it this way; "Perfect love casteth
out fear"(see 1 John 4:18). There is no fear in love.
If a Christian lives in fear, it means his love relationship with God is not what it should be. What
would we have to fear if we walked hand in hand
with Christ? If Christ showed up in bodily form, and
we walked with Him, we could walk through the
worst part of town and have nothing to fear. Our
fear would be gone because of being in the presence
of perfect love.

First John 4:8 says, "He that loveth not knoweth
not God; for God is love." We pray in error when we

pray, "God, give me love for that person." Love does not come separate from God, for God is love. Our inability to love someone is from our lack of godliness. God does not give us love apart from himself. He is love, therefore, what we need is more of God. The only way to gain more of God is to spend time in His presence.

Power

James 5:16 says, "The effectual fervent prayer of a righteous man availeth much." Prayer obviously is powerful. It's the most powerful thing there is. Prayer is the most powerful thing a believer can do, and yet it's the least practiced thing believers do. The prayer meeting is still the least attended meeting of all.

The effectual, fervent prayer of a righteous man availeth much. These two words, "effectual, fervent," make up one Greek word, *enegero*. This is where we get the word energy. This verse means that the energized prayer of a righteous man availeth much. The word "avail" means something that accomplishes much work. The verse creates a very powerful picture. There's great force in prayer.

Even though prayer is very powerful, the problem is getting people to pray. We must remember that we are not trying to get a reluctant God to do something; God is trying to get reluctant believers to pray. God is far more interested in doing things than we are in seeing them done. God is more interested in revival than we are. If we wanted what God wanted, prayer would be a much bigger part of our life.

Spiritual Awakening

Acts 1:14 says, "These all continued with one accord in prayer and supplication, with the women, and Mary the mother of Jesus, and with his brethren." Then in Acts 2:41 we read, "Then they that gladly received his word were baptized: and the same day there were added unto them about three thousand souls." This is the account of the Day of Pentecost when 3,000 souls were saved in a single meeting.

I once read an article written by the late Jamie Buckingham about an experience he had while visiting the Hoover Dam. His ordeal was very similar to one I had. When I was a little boy our family went on a vacation to the Northwest part of the United States. We visited a large dam used to produce electricity. Prior to my visit, my impression was that the water which flowed over the dam was where all of the power came from. The huge splashes it made when the water hit the rocks below were very impressive. However, the power does not come from the water that spills over the dam, even though it is quite magnificent. These structures are constructed with huge inlets at the very bottom of them. As the river rushes up the against it, it is forced through the inlets. Water deep below the surface is what turns the huge turbines which produce the electricity. The water that is involved in generating all of that power is not even visible to those on the outside. When the water pressure is too great they let water spill over the dam. That which is spilling over has really little to do with the real power, even though it gives the appearance of being quite powerful.

Within Christianity there is a drawing to anything that looks exciting. We like the splashing, we like miracles, we like accounts of demons, but the real source of power is not that which is visible to the naked eye. Short public prayer is only made powerful through long private prayer.

While walking through the structure a person can be quite taken up with an awesome sense of power. The building has a low rumble to it with a slight vibration going throughout the whole structure because of the tremendous amount of power being generated.

Reconsidering our opening verses (Acts 1:14, 2:41) when on the Day of Pentecost they were in the upper room praying. After they had prayed for some time, the Holy Spirit was poured out. "And suddenly there came a sound from heaven as of a rushing mighty wind, and it filled all the house where they were sitting" (Acts 2:2). When the Holy Spirit was poured out the building literally shook with His presence.

Prayer is the unseen thing that generates the power of God. Praying is not very attractive. There is not a lot of pomp and circumstance associated with it. However, it is the very thing that creates power. The prayer warriors are the unsung heroes of the work of God. What they do is unseen.

When they were in prayer in the Upper Room, the disciples generated such a sense of God's presence that the building shook with power. The Upper Room could no longer contain the presence of God, so it spilled out into the community. Three thousand people were saved in a single day. That's the kind of thing that would be wonderful to see again! Wouldn't we like to see the Spirit of God flowing out of our beings, touching all of the people around us with the presence of God?

Life Through Death

The kingdom of God works on this principle: life comes through death. If it were not for the death of Christ, we would not have our spiritual life today. We who have the Spirit of Christ in us are being asked to lay our lives down so that others may know the life of Christ. That is done primarily through prayer. Intercession is praying for others. When we pray for others, we are denying ourselves our own schedule, and we are denying ourselves our emotional gratification. In essence we are laying our life down so that those whom we are praying for can gain spiritual life. When Christians come together and collectively die (pray), they put light and life out into a dark world. We are putting Christ out into a dark world through our own death. When people begin to respond to that, they are naturally drawn to their source of nurture. Peter says, "Newborn babes, desire the sincere milk of the word, that ye may grow thereby" (1 Pet. 2:2). A baby desires the sincere milk of the Word. What Peter is talking about is the natural desire a baby has to feed. We don't have to teach it to be hungry. It is naturally drawn to its source of nurture.

The place of prayer becomes the source of feeding for those on a spiritual search. Our prayers (or our death) becomes a source of life in the same way Christ's death is our source of spiritual life.

Spiritual awakening has to be birthed. Giving birth is a function of the Bride, not the Groom. In that sense, when we consider Christ, the Groom, and His bride, the Church, Christ cannot give birth to spiritual awakening. Giving birth is the Church's, or the Bride's function. There's no giving birth outside of intimacy. If we lack intimacy with Christ, we are never brought to those places described as deep places of travailing. In Romans 8:26 we read about the deep kind of praying that brings us to a place of travailing:

> Likewise the Spirit also helpeth our infirmities: for we know not what we should pray for as we ought: but the Spirit itself maketh intercession for us with groanings which cannot be uttered.

"Unutterable groans" describes travailing in prayer, or giving birth in prayer. If we lack intimacy with Christ, we really are never brought to a place of giving birth through our prayers. However, when we are brought to that place where we'll lay our lives down in order to give life, we then become a source of nurture. When we lay our lives down (die to self), then the life of Christ is increased within us. His life, in us, becomes that which others feed from.

Obedience is the food, or nurturing agent, that new Christians feed from. It takes obedience to pray. It takes obedience to study the Word. It takes obedience to remain faithful to the Lord. If we want a young Christian to grow in the things of the Lord, we should couple them with a mature, obedient Christian, because their faithfulness is what the young one feeds from. Obedience in prayer is the key to intimacy with God, which in turn gives birth to spiritual awakening.

Chapter Five

Prayer Hindrances

t will be important to clarify one thing before we look into the subject of prayer hindrances. When referring to the prayer life, the author distinguishes between having prayer in your life or having a prayer life. A prayer life could also be defined as a life centered on prayer. All believers have some form of prayer in their life. It would be quite rare to find a believer who does not pray at all. However, there is a big difference between praying occasionally and having a life based on prayer.

Periodic Prayers

Periodic prayers are the result of seeing prayer as the thing that we do when we want something from God. If we pray simply out of our need, our prayer life is sporadic at best. We tend to not pray much when things are going well. When things go bad we pray. Prayer then becomes something related to difficulties. Subsequently, we pray and ask God to answer our prayers, so we can finally stop praying.

Just think of the dilemma we put God in. He wants to spend time with His children. He loves our presence similarly to how parents love the presence of their own children. When we pray, we are in His presence. If we are asking God to answer our prayers so we can finally stop praying, then we are asking Him to do something for us that will take us out of His presence.

The Prayer Life

Having a prayer life, or living a life centered around prayer, comes when we see prayer as offering ourselves to God. It's praying from a desire to be in God's presence. We become much more dependent upon him as we give more of ourselves to Him. Subsequently our entire life comes from Him. This creates an even greater need to pray, consequently, we develop a life centered on prayer. Praying then becomes the activity we draw our life from.

Guilt

Prayer hindrances are those things that keep us from developing a life of prayer. Guilt is one of the primary things that keeps us from prayer. In Psalms 40:12 the Psalmist says, "For innumerable evils have compassed me about: mine iniquities have taken hold upon me, so that I am not able to look up."

David creates the picture of hanging his head in shame. It's like saying, "I do not really want to look God in the eye for I'm so full of shame." Most of us can relate to this. Romans 3:23 says, "For all have sinned, and come short of the glory of God." On certain days we feel like we have come short of how God would have us live. It is common to have feelings of guilt. However, that should not keep us from prayer.

There are some important things for us to understand about guilt. First, God removes it. I once heard Dick Eastman say, "Condemnation kills, conviction cures." Condemnation kills the spirit while conviction cures it. If there is sin in our lives, we need to deal with it. We do need to ask God to forgive us, but we also need to come to the full understanding that when God forgives He forgets. Then He forgets that he forgave. God wipes sin out. If we still have feelings of condemnation we can rest assured that those feelings do not come from God, because God doesn't condemn, He convicts. In Romans 8:1 we read: "There is therefore now no condemnation to them which are in Christ Jesus." There is no condemnation for those who are in Christ. However, that does not mean we will never have feelings of condemnation, it means that those feelings are not from God.

God, through conviction, has the unique ability of simultaneously revealing to us our sin and drawing us to himself. If it were not for conviction, none of us would come to the Lord. Jesus said that it was to our advantage that He go away. He then said if He did not go away the Comforter would not come. He also told us that when He (the Spirit) comes, He will convict and that He convicts in three areas; in sin, in righteousness, and judgment (see John 16:8).

Jesus said that one of the primary functions of the Holy Spirit is to convict men. Conviction differs from punishment. Conviction draws us to God. God never reveals our sin for the purpose of judgment, but rather reconciliation. God is not interested in judging His people, but in reconciling His people to Him. If we refuse reconciliation, then judgment is the end result, but that is not God's heart. He does not want to judge us any more than we want to judge our children. We would much rather have a right relationship with our children then to be harsh with them.

Conviction is what draws us to God. Condemnation draws us away from God. We must always move toward God. If we need to deal with sin, then deal with sin. Always keep in mind that God forgives. If you allow guilt to keep you from prayer you fall completely into the plan of Satan. He will do everything he can to keep you from spending time with Jesus.

Worldliness

Worldliness is another great hindrance to prayer.

> Then came certain of the elders of Israel unto me, and sat before me. And the word of the Lord came unto me, saying, Son of man, these men have set up their idols in their heart, and put the

stumblingblock of their iniquity before
their face: should I be inquired of at all
by them? (Ezek. 14:1-3).

In this account the elders of Israel had come before Ezekiel. When they sat down, the Word of the
Lord came to him and told him that they had idols in
their hearts. Then God said He would not listen to
them at all, because of their idols.

Idolatry and worldliness are the same thing. We
do not often think of these things as the same. We
often think of idolatry as having little statues made
of wood or rock in our homes that we bow down to.
Most people consider that different from worldliness.
Though we may not have idols that we bow down
to, we could still be involved in idolatry. Our idols
today take on a different form. You could have an
idol sitting in the driveway outside your home. Anything that we put before the Lord is an idol or worldliness.

The root of worldliness and idolatry is pride. If
we look at the Old Testament where they dealt a lot
with idolatry, primarily idols represented sensuality.
Idolatry is primarily the worship of carnality. Most
of them were fertility gods, which makes self the basic idol. If it were not for self, these other gods would
not mean anything.

Typically, we get involved in worldliness or idolatry when we are looking to nurture our flesh. Remember, the root of worldliness is pride. It is from pride
that men look for exaltation among other men. That

is why fashion is even important to us. This is why the world gets our attention. The world is designed to exalt men above God. That is what the spirit of this world is, and our attraction to it shows us that we're in the middle of a struggle called "dying to self."

If there is even a little element of worldliness in our lives it gets in the way of prayer. In our heart-of-hearts we know the things that we put before God. If we are worldly we will not want to pray, so that God will not have the opportunity to deal with these things.

Unforgiveness

A third hindrance is unforgiveness. Mark 11:25 says, "And when ye stand praying, forgive, if ye have ought against any: that your Father also which is in heaven may forgive you your trespasses." There is a major principle in Scripture that says God forgives us to the same degree that we forgive others. The Bible is quite clear in saying that if we do not forgive others, we cannot be forgiven.

Unforgiveness is the highest form of spiritual pride there is. We cannot exalt ourselves higher than when we refuse to forgive someone else. There is a very simple reason for this. Suppose there is someone in your life who has offended you to the point that you have decided not to forgive them. One day they decide to turn from their sin, repent, and ask God to forgive them. What happens when a man genuinely repents of his sin? God forgives. In essence then, God will forgive the person we will not forgive. So what we have in unforgiveness is this — the very God of creation will forgive them, but we will not. That is an exaltation of ourselves. Through unforgiveness we are saying we have higher standards than God himself has. We are putting ourselves above Him by refusing to do for another what He would do for them.

Blasphemy

I want us to consider another aspect of unforgiveness. In Luke 12:10 we read, "And everyone who will speak a word against the Son of Man, it shall be forgiven him; but he who blasphemes against the Holy Spirit, it shall not be forgiven him." There are only two things the Bible talks about as unforgivable — blasphemy against the Holy Spirit and refusing to forgive another person. These two things are the same.

The Law of Mutual Resemblance simply says this: Scripture interprets Scripture. There has been much debate about what the unpardonable sin is. No matter what man may have concluded concerning this, let's allow Scripture to interpret Scripture. The Scripture teaches us that there are different types of sin. There are sins of the nature and sins of the will.

Sins of the Nature

My little children, these things write I unto you, that ye sin not. And if any man sin, we have an advocate with

the Father, Jesus Christ the righteous:
And he is the propitiation for our sins:
and not for ours only, but also for the
sins of the whole world (1 John 2:1-2).

John tells us not to sin, but then he says if you do happen to sin you have a covering of that sin in Jesus Christ. The type of sin that is automatically covered would be called a sin of the nature. Sins of the nature are natural (sinful) reactions we may have to something. Suppose someone is driving in a way that causes you to slam on your brakes. It's entirely possible for you to think or say something that is quite sinful. This was not premeditated sin, it was something that came from your nature. Jesus is our propitiation or covering for that sin.

Sins of the Will

Sins of the will are quite another issue. Sins of the will are deliberate, willful sins where you have full knowledge that what you're doing is sinful yet you continue to do it. There does not seem to be an automatic covering for this kind of sin because it is willful.

Continuing in 1 John 2:9 we read, "He who says he is in the light, and [yet] hates his brother, is in darkness until now." Hating, or unforgiveness, is willful. If a person dies in willful sin he is not forgiven.

Let's consider what the Book of Numbers teaches us.

And if any soul sin through ignorance, then he shall bring a she goat of
the first year for a sin offering. And
the priest shall make an atonement for
the soul that sinneth ignorantly, when
he sinneth by ignorance before the
Lord, to make an atonement for him;
and it shall be forgiven him (Num.
15:27-28).

Unintentional sin, or a sin of the nature, is covered by the priest. However, it is quite a different
outcome when the sin is deliberate:

"But anyone who sins defiantly,
whether native-born or alien,
blasphemes the Lord, and that person
must be cut off from his people.
Because he has despised the Lord's
word and broken his commands, that
person must surely be cut off; his guilt
remains on him" (Num. 15:30-
31;NIV).

There is no automatic covering for the one who
is defiant or blasphemous. It seems that the Scripture
teaches us that blasphemy of the Holy Spirit is the
willful, defiant rejection of His work on earth. If we
reject what the Holy Spirit came to do, we then attribute the work of God to Satan. Jesus was accused
of using the power of Satan to do the work of God.

The Holy Spirit's Work

What does the word "gospel" mean? It means good news! The good news is that our sins can be forgiven. The whole message of our Saviour is that He came to forgive men of their sins.

Then when He left the earth He said:

> But I tell you the truth: It is for your good that I am going away. Unless I go away, the Counselor will not come to you; but if I go, I will send him to you (John 16:7;NIV).

Why would it be to our advantage for Him to go? The answer is found when he said, "I will send Him to you." Jesus is talking about the Helper, or Holy Spirit. While Jesus was on earth, men only experienced His presence when He was physically with them. Now that He has ascended to heaven, His Holy Spirit can dwell in the hearts of men. Now millions, if not billions, can have His presence simultaneously.

Then he said in John 16:8, "When he comes, he will convict the world of guilt in regard to sin and righteousness and judgment" (NIV). The Holy Spirit was sent to convict men. Conviction reveals faults. When a person is convicted by the Holy Spirit, he is being reproved for not being like Jesus. Therefore, the entire ministry of the Holy Spirit is to teach us to live like Christ.

When a man willfully refuses to forgive another man he is knowingly rejecting, or blaspheming, the whole purpose of the Holy Spirit. The Holy Spirit's work is to remind us of the reason Jesus came to earth. He came to forgive men of their sins. When we refuse to forgive, having been forgiven, we willfully blaspheme the Holy Spirit.

The Unmerciful Servant

In Matthew 18 there is a great lesson to be learned concerning this. In this parable Jesus is teaching us that since we have been forgiven, being completely unworthy of forgiveness, we should never withhold forgiveness from another.

The king in this parable forgave a man his debt because he was not able to repay him. Then the forgiven man went out and demanded that another man pay him what he owed him. He would not forgive the other man though he himself had been forgiven. Consider the words of our Lord in this matter:

> Then the master called the servant in. "You wicked servant," he said, "I canceled all that debt of yours because you begged me to. Shouldn't you have had mercy on your fellow-servant just as I had on you?" In anger his master turned him over to the jailers to be tortured, until he should pay back all he owed. "This is how my heavenly

Father will treat each of you unless you
forgive your brother from your heart"
(Matt. 18:32-35;NIV).

Real Emotions

Being human, we deal with real emotions. If we
come to the Lord and say, "I know that I'm supposed
to forgive this person, but I just cannot right now."
That is not going to shock the Lord. He knows that
about us already. God is not afraid of truth. However, until we come to the place of admitting our feelings, we cut off the Holy Spirit's ability to bring us
into true forgiveness. We will not receive help until
we express our need for it.

Confessing our inability to forgive is also expressing our need for God to help us. When we pray, "Lord,
I'm willing to be made willing," we bring ourselves
to the place where the Lord can work with us. He can
bring us to the place where the forgiveness is genu-
ine.

We have to forgive. We really have no other option. This is a part of what we pray in the Lord's
prayer: forgive us our sins as we forgive our debtors.
What we are saying in essence is, if we do not forgive others, God does not have to forgive us.

First John 4:8 says, "He that loveth not knoweth
not God; for God is love." How many people, that
don't know God, are going to heaven? If there is an
element of unforgiveness in us it really hinders prayer.
We cannot draw close to God and remain bitter to-

ward those whom God loves. It's just impossible, because to love God is to love others. If we are going to get close to God, we are going to have to make right our relationships with other men. Once taken care of, then the avenue to pray completely opens to us.

Chapter Six

Prayer Problems

here are a number of things that present themselves as problems to prayer. We will look at two of those in this chapter.

One of those problems is that of unanswered prayer. Habakkuk 1:2 refers to a time when the prophet had been in prayer, and he didn't really see God answering him, so he said, "O Lord, how long shall I cry, and thou wilt not hear!"

It is not uncommon to think that God has not heard our prayer. Many times Satan will say, "Why pray for that? You prayed before and it wasn't answered. Why pray again?" We must keep one thing in mind when it comes to Satan. He is a liar (see John 8:44). He never speaks the truth to us. Therefore, when he tries to tell us that it's useless to pray, we should understand that the opposite of what he says is true. We should pray all the harder.

Unanswered prayer is not nearly as big of a problem as unrecognized answers are. Even the prophet Habakkuk experienced this. If we were to read through his book, we would find that God did answer his prayer, but it came later, and it came in a way that he didn't expect. God told the prophet to keep praying, but at the same time he would have to wait. He told him that the answer to his prayer would come at an appointed time.

> For the vision is yet for an appointed time, but at the end it shall speak, and not lie: though it tarry, wait for it; because it will surely come, it will not tarry (Hab. 2:3).

God answers every prayer, but in many cases we have such narrow vision of what God is doing that we fail to see the greater picture. We struggle when God answers our prayers in a way which is different from how we prayed. We feel that we have prayed in the most effective way — and therefore that God should answer according to our "effective" request. However, God often answers our prayers in ways that bring more glory to Him than if He would have answered it our way.

God does not take away a man's free will. Because of that, God gains an opportunity to do much more when we pray than we realize. Prayer does not make a puppet out of a person. When we begin to pray for someone, it doesn't mean that soon that person's life will be manipulated by God. God won't remove the free will because that would violate the nature of a relationship.

The beauty of a relationship is the free will. The beauty of my wife's relationship with me is that she has the freedom to walk away from me, but she chooses to stay with me. Suppose my wife wanted to leave me, but I was a manipulator, and I had so arranged things in my wife's life that even though she wanted to leave me she couldn't. Where would the beauty of our relationship be?

The beauty of our relationship with Christ is the fact that we have the freedom to walk away from Him, but we choose to stay with Him. The only people who go to heaven will be those who had the freedom to sin but chose to obey God instead.

When we begin to pray for someone, the Holy Spirit gains a freedom to arrange the circumstances of that person's life in order to make it easy to accept the Lord. If you start praying for a man, the issue of his salvation regularly comes before him. He is continually brought to a place of decision. At the point of decision, if he refuses to accept the Lord, then the Holy Spirit goes back to work to bring him to another point of decision. As long as a man is being prayed for, he will be faced with this issue over and over.

Job 33:28-30 says, "He will deliver his soul from going into the pit, and his life shall see the light. Lo, all these things worketh God oftentimes with man, To bring back his soul from the pit, to be enlightened with the light of the living." In verse 29 it says in essence, God will work in a man's life, time and time again in order to enlighten him.

Our problem is that we think that we know how God is working in someone's life, and so we assume too much. Then, when it doesn't happen the way we assumed, we interpret it as an unanswered prayer. One day I received a phone call from a lady who had been praying for her husband's salvation for a long time. She said to me, "I've been praying for my husband for so long and nothing is happening. God is not answering this prayer." We began to discuss her dilemma, and as we did, the Lord began to show her some things. From the time that she began to pray for her husband, all of his closest friends had come to know Jesus Christ. Every time she would talk to her husband about the things of God, he would say to her, "If I give my life to Christ, all of my friends will make fun of me." Now that all of his friends are Christians, it could be that if he doesn't give his life to Christ soon, all of his friends might make fun of him, at least in his thinking. God has simply been at work arranging the circumstances of his life so as to make it easier for him to submit to Christ.

When we pray for someone, the Lord gains a freedom to affect all sorts of things, even though we may be praying primarily for one thing. Suppose the Lord was limited to only responding to us according to the way we pray. Half of the time we don't even pray for our own family, much less our community or our country. Because of the free will, God can take the prayers for one man and can actually affect all sorts of things. In this lady's case, God took her prayers for her husband and brought about the salvation of several other men.

God is doing much more than we realize. The Word of God tells us to pray. Therefore, God fully intends to answer prayer. God has purpose in all that He does. When He prompts us to prayer, it's because He intends to answer our prayer. We need to broaden our perspective and gain a greater picture of what the Lord is doing when we pray.

God Answers in Four Ways

Traditionally, we have viewed answered prayer in three ways. We say God answers with a "yes," a "no," and a "wait." Those answers may be a little simplistic, but they are nonetheless true. There are times when everything is in order, and when we pray, the answer is quick. John 15:7 says, "If ye abide in me, and my words abide in you, ye shall ask what ye will, and it shall be done unto you." To "abide" means to walk as Christ walked (see 1 John 2:6). When we abide, the very thing we pray for will be answered with a "yes."

It is possible to get a "no," also. If we pray completely contrary to the will of God, we cannot expect an answer. Isaiah 1:15 teaches us this very thing: "And when ye spread forth your hands, I will hide mine eyes from you: yea, when ye make many prayers, I will not hear: your hands are full of blood." When a person's hands are full of blood, it means there is sin in his life and that his motives in prayer are out of order.

I have had more than one occasion where someone in a church has come up to me and said, "God has finally led me to the love of my life, so — pray that I can divorce my mate." What they're saying is, "I'm in an affair, and I need to get out of my marriage." When our request is so contrary to the Word of God, we can expect an answer to come in the form of a "no."

In chapter 2, we discussed the times when God will wait before answering a prayer because of timing or other situations that we may not even be able to see. In Luke 18 we have an example where Jesus begins the chapter saying that men should always pray and not give up. Then in verse 7, he says, "And shall not God avenge his own elect, which cry day and night unto him, though he bear long with them?" When the verse says, "though he bear long with them," it's talking about the fact that God may not answer the prayer right away but that He will ultimately answer it.

There is a fourth way that God answers prayer, and that's with a "do-it-yourself." I once heard Dick Eastman talk about this very issue. It is not uncommon to ask God to do many things that He may want us to do. I have heard people pray, "God, send a good Christian to witness to my neighbor." That is the type of prayer where God may very well say, "Do it yourself." The problem with prayer is that the pray-er becomes the candidate for the answer of every prayer he ever prays. If we pray long enough for someone, pretty soon we are the one carrying the burden for them. After we have prayed long enough concerning a situation, we start saying, "I need to do something about this."

There was a little boy who was listening to his dad praying in the living room. His dad was praying, "Lord, our neighbor has lost his job, and he's going to need help, he's going to need food, he's going to need finances, etc., etc." While the dad was going down this list, his little four-year-old boy left the room and went into the kitchen. After a little while he came back into the room with a bag and his dad asked him, "What do you have there?"

The little boy responded, "I got this bag!"

His father said, "What's in it?"

When he opened up the bag, he found a bunch of groceries. He said to his boy, "Where are you going with this?"

The little boy said, "Well, I'm going to the neighbors to answer your prayer. You said they need food, and we have food."

Prayer is the chief thing we do, but it can't be the only thing we do. It has to be pre-eminent, but it can't be all that we do.

Insincere Prayer

In James 4:2 we read, "Yet ye have not, because ye ask not." That's a simple verse to understand. If something is as simple as asking for it and receiving it, then it is something that is in the will of God. Contextually that is true, also. James is dealing with something that God wills for us to have. So in essence He's saying, the only reason you don't have this thing is because you have not asked for it. Then in the next verse it says, "Ye ask, and receive not, because ye ask amiss, that ye may consume it upon your lusts" (James 4:3). The little phrase, "you ask amiss," means you have wrong motives when you're praying. This is very interesting because right after saying that all we have to do to receive this particular thing is to ask for it, he says in essence, when you ask for it, you don't receive it because your motives are out of order. Do you know what James is saying? He's saying that there are things that could be in the center of the will of God, and yet when we pray for them, He will not answer. This teaches us that God is as interested in the pray-er as He is in what we are praying for.

It seems that believers today have tried to separate themselves from any personal responsibility or maturity. We try to separate who we are from God's work. We have come to believe that God's work is a mechanical operation. We seem to think that God is obligated to respond to our praying as long as we pray correctly. We are inclined to forget that this is a relationship and that the work of God is accomplished by who we are, not just by what we do. God is more interested in working in us than He is in working through us. We have a tendency to forget that we are here to reflect the Son of God. If God were to answer our prayers while we have wrong motives we would tend to never feel the need to become more like Christ.

We could be in the center of the will of God and not see an answer to our prayers if we are praying with the wrong motives. Wrong motives tend to be self-centered motives. We could be praying for something that God actually wants to accomplish, but if we ask simply so our situation will get better, then we have wrong motives.

We sometimes operate under the false impression that if something is God's will, then it is going to be accomplished no matter what it is. That is not so. Knowing the will of God is simply to help us pray the way God wants us to pray. However, praying is more than simply an act. We must pray with right motives before we can reflect the heart of Christ.

We know that it is the will of God to save all men. Second Peter 3:9 says, "The Lord is not slack concerning his promise, as some men count slackness; but is longsuffering toward us, not willing that any should perish, but that all should come to repentance." Just because it is God's will for all men to be saved does not mean that all men will automatically be saved. If that were the case, we would not need to be evangelistic at all. If that were the case, Christ would not have given us the Great Commission.

Knowing what His will is helps us to pray correctly. When I was a youth pastor, I used to hear the young girls pray this prayer quite often, "God, save my boyfriend so my parents will finally like him." It's a right prayer insomuch as God wants to save the boyfriends. However, they were praying for their boyfriends' salvation for their own sake. They wanted him to get saved so their own relationship with their parents would get better.

We should pray for the salvation of any man — it doesn't matter who it is — for one reason: so that their salvation will bring glory to God. We are not to pray for their salvation so that it will ease our situation. A lady once asked me to pray for the salvation of her husband because she said she needed peace in her home. That's a wrong motive! Jesus is the Prince of Peace. When He comes into someone's heart, peace will be the result. What she was saying in essence was this, "We're so tired of living with turmoil and tension that I want God to save him so that our lifestyle will be better." The danger in this is that we put our desires before Him, and we start praying for a situation without remembering the glory of God. We forget that men are to be saved because their salvation will bring glory to the One who has died for them. There will be peace, there will be happiness, there will be all those things as the result of them getting saved.

Checking our motives is such an important thing for us to do. Psalm 139:23 says, "Search me, O God, and know my heart: try me, and know my thoughts." If we don't have a daily practice of saying, "God look into my heart," we can get all wrapped up in things that have ulterior motives. It's healthy to daily pray and say, "Lord, what are the motives of my heart?" This is the single most important point of this book.

It is possible to be praying in the center of God's will and not see an answer. Prayer changes the pray-er, more than the things you pray for. Prayer changes things, obviously, but generally those things that are changed come through the changes prayer brings into the heart of the one who is praying.

Chapter Seven

Prayer Excuses

e will now look at some prayer excuses and the reasons we give God for not praying. We must understand that everyone lives by the same rule. We all do what is important to us. Our lives are structured around the things we consider important. The reason you are reading this book while others may never read it is because prayer is important to you. By this reasoning, we can safely conclude one thing: When God is important enough to us, the end result will be prayer.

Too Tired

The most common excuse is, "I'm too tired to pray." Have any of you ever fallen asleep in prayer? Ephesians 5:14 has some advice for us; it says, "Awaken, thou that sleepest and arise!" That verse is taken out of context, but it does make sense. If you should fall asleep while praying, then pray when you wake up again. I don't know of any other activity that is curtailed by weariness as much as prayer is. We can be weary and do almost anything — except pray. I've been dead-tired and yet driven my car across whole states, but if I'm a little tired when it comes to prayer time, I'm out in a flash. One of the best ways to cure insomnia is to pray! On the night you can't sleep, get out of bed and get on your knees and start praying — and your insomnia will be cured instantly.

Being tired is really common. I don't believe anyone can do anything to solve that dilemma in our lives, because the only cure for being tired is sleep. What I want to do is show how we can still spend time in prayer despite our weariness. If we allow weariness to keep us from prayer, we will always be kept from prayer because we always seem to be weary when it comes to prayer. There are three things that can help us in this issue.

1. Give God the best time of the day.

What I mean by the best time of the day is when we can be the most effective and that may differ from person to person. I have always been more of a morning person. I don't mind getting up early. I kind of like that. My wife differs from me. She is a night person, she is better off praying after she has been up for a while.

We should not get religious about this issue. We're not going to get more done for God by getting up early in the morning to pray and then finding ourselves falling back to sleep during our prayer time. If a person can pray in the afternoon or in the evening and have a good solid prayer time, they will get much more done for God that way. "Resting in the Lord" just doesn't accomplish all that much when it means we're asleep.

In the Bible we see that God's people prayed at various times during the day. We see David who said, "When I remember thee upon my bed, and meditate on thee in the night watches" (Ps. 63:6). David would often pray at night. He knew the importance of putting God before everything. Jesus also prayed at night. "And it came to pass in those days, that he went out into a mountain to pray, and continued all night in prayer to God" (Luke 6:12).

"And Abraham got up early in the morning to the place where he stood before the Lord" (Gen. 19:27). Abraham had a morning place where he stood (prayed) before the Lord. "O God, thou art my God; early will I seek thee: my soul thirsteth for thee" (Ps. 63:1).

It was a common practice to go to the temple and pray in the ninth hour, which was 3:00 p.m. "Now Peter and John went up together into the temple at the hour of prayer, being the ninth hour" (Acts 3:1).

Daniel prayed at three different times each day, morning, noon, and night. "Now when Daniel knew that the writing was signed, he went into his house; and his windows being open in his chamber toward Jerusalem, he kneeled upon his knees three times a day, and prayed, and gave thanks before his God, as he did aforetime" (Dan. 6:10).

2. Pray audibly.

Falling asleep in prayer comes from thinking our prayers. Praying silently is a legitimate type of prayer. "And God saw . . . every imagination of the thoughts of his heart" (Gen. 6:5). However, if you are falling asleep while you are trying to think your prayers, then pray audibly instead. That which precedes falling asleep is called "daydreaming," and typically we don't start daydreaming when we are talking audibly. Praying audibly keeps us focused.

3. Pace.

If a person is struggling with drowsiness they should get up and move around. Pacing is different than just going for a walk and thinking about God. It's deliberate. It's walking back and forth. When I first began to pray, I determined in my heart that if I started to fall asleep, I would get up and move around. I have become so comfortable with pacing that I do my best praying that way. It just keeps me focused. It keeps me intense. A lack of intensity means wandering thoughts. The more focused a person is, the less they deal with wandering thoughts and things that frustrate us in our prayer time. Remember: "And Enoch walked with God" (Gen. 5:22).

Too Busy

Another excuse is, "I'm too busy to pray." Ephesians 5:15-16 says, "See then that ye walk circumspectly, not as fools, but as wise, Redeeming the time, because the days are evil." Paul talks about two types of men. There is the fool and there is the wise man. He says the fool does not redeem his time; the wise man does. The word "redeem" in the Greek *exagorazo* which means "purchase out of the market place." In Paul's time the market place was where all the activity of the day took place. Today it would signify your job or the world. It's that which you give your life to. We are advised in this verse (16) to purchase back time from the world. The world will take all of our time if we allow it. The wise man, in other words, will purchase time to pray. The fool will say, "I'm too busy to pray." Paul didn't say, "The wise man has a whole bunch of time, and that's why he prays." He says that the wise man will purchase, he will buy back from the world, time for prayer.

We need to develop an attitude about time that is similar to the one we have about money. The same principles apply to both. The more time you give God, the more time you have from God. It is not any easier to explain how God does this than it is to explain how God increases our finances if we pay our tithes. All we really know is that if we are faithful in our tithes and offerings, God is faithful. Our bills are always met. God increases what we give to Him. If we will give God the time we do have, God will give us more.

I began praying when I was a seminary student. I would be in classes from 7:30 a.m. until noon or 1:00 p.m. Then I would drive 45 minutes to get home. I would then have from about 2:00 p.m. until midnight (10 hours) to do my studies, be with my wife, and sleep. At midnight I would go to work and then get off of work at 6:00 a.m. That did not give me any "extra" time. It was in the midst of that hectic schedule that God began to deal with me about my prayer life. I didn't know where I would gain any time for praying. I began to give the Lord the little time I did have. After a while, I found that I had more time to pray. Soon I was giving Him at least an hour and a half each day, and then two hours each day. Today I have a lifestyle that allows me all the time I want for prayer.

I did not share that with you to say that I'm exceptional. The point I want to make is that I simply followed the principle of sowing and reaping. God will give back what you give to Him, and then He increases it. I believe most people are very busy, but I don't believe that we are too busy to pray. In fact, the Bible doesn't address this as being, "Busy or not." It addresses it as being, "foolish or not." The wise man will pay a price to pray; the fool will not. The wise man may find himself going to bed an hour later than normal in order to find time to pray. He may find himself getting out of bed an hour earlier in order to find time to pray. Our wisdom will drive us to this. Our foolishness will keep us away from it.

Too Dry

Another excuse is "I'm too dry." Or, "I just don't feel like praying." If we wait until we feel like praying, we would pray very little. Luke 18:1 states, "Then Jesus told his disciples a parable to show them that they should always pray and not give up." And the word, "should" is an act of the will. In other words,

Jesus says that men, by an act of their will, should pray. We cannot wait until we feel led to pray before we actually pray. Certainly we should pray every time we feel led to pray, but for the most part, we lead ourselves to prayer. Ninety percent of the prayer life is simply making ourselves do it. There's nothing mystical about this. It's work. It's spiritual discipline.

Some people think that because I have a prayer ministry that I don't struggle with the things other people struggle with. That's simply not true. When my alarm goes off in the morning, I don't float out of bed and then float to a place of prayer and just have some kind of ecstatic moment. Neither do I jump out of bed and say, "Praise God, I was tired of sleeping anyway." Typically, I stumble out of bed, and I stumble to a place of prayer. Sometimes I make myself wake up before I pray. There are times when I'll shower before I pray just to wake myself up.

The sports shoe manufacturer, Nike, had a famous slogan: "Just do it!" They were trying to get people to exercise and subsequently to buy their shoes. It's interesting that the Nike company used this as their slogan. Nike comes from the Greek word, *nakao*, which means "overcomer." Our military named one of its missiles "the Nike missile." The Nike was a missile that could be fired after another missile had already been launched. The Nike missile could catch up with the first missile and overcome it. If we want to be overcomers in the area of prayer then we must "Just do it!"

Too Lazy

Another favorite excuse is "I'm too lazy" to pray. This is not something we readily admit to. I have never been a part of a testimony service in a church where someone stood up and said, "I just want to thank God for my lazy spirit." I have known people who have wanted to stand up to testify to this very thing but couldn't actually bring themselves to standing up. I think in many ways laziness is the primary excuse.

Prayer itself is not very difficult. We will never really run out of things to pray for. If we have a very simplistic approach to prayer we could spend more time in prayer than we really have time for. Suppose we were to think of 12 people that need prayer and spend five minutes praying for each person. Praying for 12 people, spending five minutes in prayer for each, will take one hour. Having plenty of things to pray for really is not the problem. The thing we struggle with the most is the decision to pray. Once we are in the place of prayer, it's not that difficult to pray. We struggle more with actually getting ourselves in that position than anything else. Getting up out of the easy chair, turning off the TV and putting ourselves in a position to pray is where most of the battle lies. Once we're in prayer, we can easily give ourselves to it. The decision to pray is the battle. Once that decision has been made, most of the battle is over.

Chapter Eight

Spiritual Warfare

atan has a plan:

> Put on the whole armour of God, that ye may be able to stand against the wiles of the devil. For we wrestle not against flesh and blood, but against principalities, against powers, against the rulers of the darkness of this world, against spiritual wickedness in high places (Eph. 6:11-12).

We should put on the whole armor of God so that we can stand against the wiles of the devil. The word "wiles" is the Greek word *methodeia* which is translated "method" or "plan." *Methodeia* is derived from the Greek word *meta* which means "against." Therefore, it is safe to say that Satan has a plan that is designed to go against God's plan.

Satan's plan is a personalized plan. The enemy knows how to discourage us or stand in opposition to us in ways that may not bother another person. I may struggle with something that just wouldn't make any sense to you at all. You may struggle with certain issues that may make no sense to me at all.

Regardless of the enemy's plan, Jesus said, "And I say also unto thee, That thou art Peter, and upon this rock I will build my church; and the gates of hell shall not prevail against it" (Matt. 16:18).

Satan's plan is not really important. What he is putting together is not nearly as important as what God is doing. Our call is to follow the Lord and to pursue Christ. Let Satan plan all that he wants. In Numbers 23:23 we read, "Surely there is *no* enchantment against Jacob, *neither is there any divination* against Israel" (emphasis added). This verse tells us that there is no plan or curse that can fall on a child of God.

Proverbs 26:2 says the same thing in essence, "As the bird by wandering, as the swallow by flying, *so the curse causeless shall not come*" (emphasis added).

As believers, we don't have to live in fear of what the followers of Satan may be doing. People are getting reports that Satanists are fasting and praying for the demise of believers. Personally, I think that it's good that they are not eating. Let them starve all they want. If we believers live in obedience to God, nothing they plan can actually cause us to lose our salvation. Paul the apostle put it this way:

Who shall separate us from the love of Christ? shall tribulation, or dis-

tress, or persecution, or famine, or na-
kedness, or peril, or sword? As it is
written, For thy sake we are killed all
the day long; we are accounted as sheep
for the slaughter. Nay, in all these things
we are more than conquerors through
him that loved us. For I am persuaded,
that neither death, nor life, nor angels,
nor principalities, nor powers, nor
things present, nor things to come, Nor
height, nor depth, nor any other crea-
ture, shall be able to separate us from
the love of God, which is in Christ Jesus
our Lord (Rom. 8:35-39).

God is greater than any plan Satan may have.
However, Satan does plan and he does scheme, and
what we have to understand is that a scheme is hidden, not outward. The enemy is free to use trickery.
He is the Father of lies, he can do anything he wants,
even if it's unethical.

Suppose Satan came up to us and said, "I just
wanted to let you know that I've got this plan. If
you yield to my temptations and fall into this plan,
it will be great for me because I'll be able to mess
up your life." If he came up to us and said it that
way, we would rebuke him. We'd stand up against
him. However, that's not how he works. He's the
Father of Lies and he's a schemer. Therefore, we
need discernment.

Discernment

Discernment is our greatest weapon in spiritual battle. If we cannot discern, we could be subject to Satan's schemes and fall right into his traps. One of the schemes that the enemy uses is to get believers to fight against him, rather than to pursue Christ. Exalting Christ automatically opposes the enemy. When we exalt Christ, all men are drawn to Him. If Satan can get our eyes off of Christ and get them on him, then he has tricked us and we have fallen prey to his scheme. We need a deep personal prayer life if for no other reason than to discern.

> And Jesus went into the temple of God, and cast out all them that sold and bought in the temple, and overthrew the tables of the moneychangers, and the seats of them that sold doves, And said unto them, It is written, My house shall be called the house of prayer; but ye have made it a den of thieves. And the blind and the lame came to him in the temple; and he healed them (Matt. 21:12-14).

In verse 13, Christ is making prayer pre-eminent by His statement, "My house will be called a house of prayer." He's saying prayer should stand over and above all of the things in the house of God, and if prayer is not pre-eminent, then the house of God robs God through her inability to discern.

Thieves in God's House

Christ was doing much more than just throwing moneychangers out of the temple. They were supposed to be there. The moneychangers were placed in the outer courts of the temple so that when the people would come to worship God from other countries, they could exchange their money for the currency accepted by the priests for the paying of the tithe. So the moneychangers were there to change money. The worshippers would also purchase their sacrifices from the moneychangers. The problem was not that moneychangers were in God's house. The problem was that they were thieves. They were robbing God's people. That is what Christ is against. Contextually, when Christ said, "My house shall be a house of prayer," He was addressing the issue of discernment more so than simply the issue of moneychangers. There were thieves in the house of God and nobody discerned it. Christianity is full of thieves today, and it seems that for the most part nobody knows it. Without prayer, we lose the ability to discern.

Christ, the Standard

Discernment needs a standard. Christ is the standard. Everything is to be measured up to His nature and character. If we are not spending enough time in

His presence, then we lose our ability to distinguish between His nature and all others. We discern a lot more than we realize. Women are much better at this than men. If a woman was given an assignment to go and purchase a dress for her mother, she could go to the dress store and look at a rack of dresses and say, "This one is Mom! I can see her in this." She may then turn to another dress and say, "This one is not mom at all." What she is doing is simply discerning which dress would be best for her mom. Her discernment is based on what she knows of her mother's character. In this case, the mother is the standard. Discernment is simply comparing that which we see to what we understand the standard to be. In the case of a woman picking out a dress for her mother, she is simply comparing what she sees in the dresses to who she understands her mother to be. Why would this work? It's because of all the time she has spent in her mother's presence. Due to the time she has spent in her presence, she can discern things based on who she knows her mother to be.

In spiritual matters Christ is our standard. In Deuteronomy 13, Moses established the theological norm for all of the Old Testament prophets. Basically they all had to be 100 percent correct. If they claimed to be a prophet then whatever they prophesied or said "in the name of the Lord" had to come true or else they were not a prophet. In the New Testament, Christ becomes that standard. He is now the theological norm. Everything that is given in a word of prophecy or anything that is given in the name of Christ has to be measured up against who Jesus is. If a prophecy does not line up with the character and nature of Christ, it has to be refuted. However, if we are not people of prayer, if we are not spending time in the presence of the Lord, then we fail to have a real living sense of His nature. If we don't know Jesus as well as we know our own parents, then if anybody quotes a Bible verse, we assume they must be right because we don't have the ability to distinguish between the spirit of the "prophet" and the spirit of Christ.

I was once talking with a person who had received some questionable advice from a "prophetess." There was a woman traveling around claiming to be a prophetess. A woman approached her with a problem asking for her advice. The woman was wanting to divorce her husband. She said that when she married her husband he promised to supply her with whatever she wanted so that she could continue to live in the style she was accustomed. The woman grew up in a very wealthy family and wanted to continue to live that way, but her husband's income could not support her lifestyle.

The "prophetess" thought about her dilemma for a while, and then she gave her some advice that she claimed was from God. She said, "God wants you happy. Therefore, you have the freedom to divorce your husband and find someone else who can make you happy." The advice of this "prophetess" must be refuted because it is completely contrary to both the nature of Christ and the Word of God. However, since the one seeking the advice did not know the Word of God, and had not spent adequate time in the presence of Christ, she felt she had no other option but to believe that the prophetess's advice was from God.

Understanding Christ's nature comes through spending time in His presence. Whenever we stop praying we lose our ability to discern. If we don't have the ability to discern, we become subject to Satan's schemes. The primary reason the Church today is obsessed with studying the enemy is that we are a relatively prayerless Church. Satan has gained much ground. However, the key to building the Kingdom of God does not lie in understanding Satan as much as it does in pursuing Christ.

Chapter Nine

Satan's Purpose

atan has a purpose.

> Then said he unto me, Fear not, Daniel: for from the first day that thou didst set thine heart to understand, and to chasten thyself before thy God, thy words were heard, and I am come for thy words. But the prince of the kingdom of Persia withstood me one and twenty days: but, lo, Michael, one of the chief princes, came to help me; and I remained there with the kings of Persia (Dan. 10:12-13).

In this account Daniel had been praying for 21 days. The answer to his prayer was delayed by spiritual battle. The demon prince of the kingdom of Persia was hindering God's angel from bringing Daniel the answer. Satan's purpose in this case was to discourage Daniel so that he would quit praying.

To understand Satan's purpose, we need to understand our Lord's. Jesus wants to get married. He spends all of His time in the preparation of His Bride. The preparation of the Bride is what the work of God is all about. The more mature the believers are, the more glorious the Bride is. Prayer is one of the primary practices in preparing or maturing the Bride. While we are in the presence of Christ, we conform to His image. If the enemy can discourage us and keep us from praying, he will do just that.

Satan's objective is to hinder the Bride. He does not want us preparing ourselves for the return of Christ. He does not want us to take on the nature of a Bride. The Bride is to have a natural longing for her groom. Revelation 22:20 says, "Even so, come, Lord Jesus." "Come Lord Jesus" is the call of the true bride of Christ. Any bride in waiting lives in anticipation of the groom.

When I was discipling a group of college-aged young people, many of the couples in our group were engaged to be married. There was one particular engaged couple who I remember very well. Jim was in college, and Karen, his fiancee, was attending our group. You could approach Karen at anytime and say, "When's the next time Jim is coming home?" and she would know exactly. She lived in anticipation of his return. How excited would Jim have been if his fiancee had not known his schedule? What if she would have answered, "Well, I haven't really thought about when he is returning next. It's possible that he's home now. I need to check this out."

That's contrary to the nature of a bride.

First John 3:3 says, "And every man that hath this hope in him purifieth himself, even as he is pure." Knowing that Christ could come at any time helps keep us from the world. The further we get away from thinking that He might come soon, the more we get involved in the world, and the more we live with the thought that we've got plenty of time to prepare for His return. Not only is that dangerous, it's contrary to the nature of a bride. Don't let Satan fulfill his purpose by distracting us from being prepared.

Satan's Persistence

Judges 16 chronicles the account of Samson and Delilah. Before we consider this particular record, we need to look at some background concerning Samson. When he was born, his parents dedicated him as a Nazarite (see Judges 13:7). In Numbers 6, the details of the Nazarite vow are laid out. Three things make up the Nazarite vow. The first is that he is to have nothing to do with the grape. He is to abstain from any kind of wine or anything that has to do with the grape. Second, he is to not cut his hair. Third, he is not to touch a dead body. Samson was to live as a Nazarite. If we take a close look at Samson's life we see a dangerous pattern. Samson got caught up with this idea of finding out all that he could do and still be strong. This is very typical of someone who has come to depend on his own ability. Samson was very powerful physically, but the true source of his strength came from keeping his vow. Samson wanted to put his strength to the test. He had a pattern of trying different things simply to see if he could handle them. He wanted to find out what all he could do and still be strong.

Today's New Testament equivalent is a philosophy that comes in the form of the question, "What all can I do and still be saved?" Believers seem to be interested in finding out what they can do and still make it to heaven. This is contrary to the nature of a relationship. In a relationship, this attitude would be tragic. We should not say, "God what all can I do in the world and still make it to heaven?" That would be very similar to a man saying to his wife, "I love you. I want you to know that I love you. But, tell me, how many other women can I be with before you divorce me? I don't want a divorce, but I would like to mess around. So how many affairs can I have?"

If a man had that approach to his wife she would probably say, "I thought you were in this relationship to see what you could do to make it better, not just to keep it barely in existence!" That is exactly the same logic we are using when we say to God, "What can I do in the world and still make it to heaven?"

Samson was caught up with this attitude. He began by going to the Valley of Timnath. The Valley of Timnath was known as the "Valley of the Grape," a prominent association with the fruit from which he was to abstain. Then he started dating a girl whose father was the keeper of the vineyard. He eventually married this girl. However, this girl, her valley, and her home were off limits to him, because he was to have no association with anything that had to do with the grape. Samson was determined to be with this girl, so he took his parents to visit her.

> Then went Samson down, and his father and his mother, to Timnath, and came to the vineyards of Timnath: and, behold, a young lion roared against him. And the spirit of the Lord came mightily upon him, and he rent him as he would have rent a kid, and he had nothing in his hand: but he told not his father or his mother what he had done (Judg. 14:5-6).

I find it quite interesting that even though Samson had full knowledge that what he was about to do was wrong and that it was in full violation of his vow as a Nazarite, yet the Spirit of the Lord came upon him mightily and he killed the lion with his bare hands. This experience got Samson thinking, *Maybe I'm special. Maybe because of my circumstances, God is going to allow sin in my life. Look how God is using me even though I have been disobedient to Him.*

Later Samson was walking down the path he had taken earlier, and he turned to look at the carcass of the lion he had killed earlier. "And after a time he returned to take her, and he turned aside to see the carcass of the lion: and, behold, there was a swarm of bees and honey in the carcass of the lion" (Judg. 14:8). The dead body of the lion was off-limits to Samson. He was a Nazarite. He was to touch no dead body, but he saw the honey. The dead body of the lion represents the things that we put to death when we gave our lives to Christ. It represents our old life. The Bible says that when you gave your life to Christ, the old passed away and all things became new (see 2 Cor. 5:17). The past is off-limits to us as believers. However, if we gaze on the past long enough, we will see the sweetness of sin. Samson saw the honey.

Hebrews teaches us that there is a certain sweetness to sin: "Choosing rather to suffer affliction with the people of God, than to enjoy the *pleasures of sin for a season*" (Heb. 11:25, emphasis added). Sin satisfies the flesh. However, it is very short-lived, and it's not satisfying on a long-term basis. Subsequently, we constantly indulge in more sin because its sweetness runs out quickly. Samson looked upon the honey so long that he could not resist, then he reached in and grabbed the honey. This caused him to touch the dead carcass. Having violated two parts of his vow to God, Samson began to think, *I can sin and still be strong.* Then he met Delilah, who depicts the persistence of Satan. If the enemy finds an area that we will play with, he will not back off. Satan will push us to the edge, then he'll push us over the edge. Then he'll kick us while we're down.

> And the lords of the Philistines came up unto her, and said unto her, Entice him, and see wherein his great strength lieth, and by what means we may prevail against him, that we may bind him to afflict him: and we will give thee every one of us eleven hundred pieces of silver (Judg. 16:5).

Delilah went to Samson and said, "Tell me, I pray thee, wherein thy great strength lieth, and wherewith thou mightest be bound to afflict thee" (Judg. 16:6). By now, Samson was deeply entrenched in this lifestyle of playing with sin and finding out what he could do and remain strong. So when Delilah tempted him, he gave in.

She asked, "Where's your strength?"

He replied, "If they bind me with seven green thongs that were never dried, then shall I be weak, and be as another man" (Judg. 16:7). So while he slept, she bound him. However, when he awakened he was still strong. Delilah came to him a second time and said, "Where is your strength?" He answered, "If they bind me fast with new ropes that never were occupied, then shall I be weak, and be as another man" (Judg. 16:11). While he slept, she tied him up with new ropes and yet when he awakened, he was still strong. Then Delilah came to him a third time and said, "Where's your strength?"

He said, "If thou weavest the seven locks of my

head with the web" (Judg. 16:13).

Every time Samson played with sin, his resistance to it grew weaker. Now, he allowed her to get right to the source of his vulnerability. The more we play with sin, the less we can resist. "And it came to pass, when she pressed him daily with her words, and urged him, so that his soul was vexed unto death" (Judg. 16:16). Samson could no longer resist. "He told her all his heart, and said, There hath not come a razor upon mine head; for I have been a Nazarite unto God from my mother's womb: if I be shaven, then my strength will go from me, and I shall become weak, and be like any other man" (Jud. 16:17).

This time, while he slept, she cut his hair. That was the final blow. Now Samson had violated all three facets of his vow, and his strength was taken. His strength was not in his hair as much as it was in his vow. Now that he has violated his vow, there was no strength left, because there was no separation. Our strength in the Lord is in our separation from the world. Do we want to find a powerless Christian? Find a worldly Christian. Do we want to find a powerful Christian? Find a holy Christian, one who is separated. Our only strength against the enemy lies in our submission to God, which results in separation, or holiness. If we are not in submission to God, then we don't have the ability to resist. If we don't resist the enemy, he will persist. Our only option is to live in submission to God.

Consider this picture. Delilah was no match for

Samson. When we compare their relative strength, Samson could have knocked Delilah into next week. The Bible also promises us superior strength when it says, "Ye are of God, little children, and have over-come them: because greater is he that is in you, than he that is in the world" (1 John 4:4). Christ in us is greater than Satan. If we were simply to compare strength to strength, Christ could destroy the enemy with a word. If we look at Samson as a believer and Delilah as the enemy, Delilah could not do a thing to Samson that he did not allow her to do. However, Delilah became the one who stole the great power of Samson because he would not stop playing with sin. James 4:7 says, "Submit yourselves therefore to God. Resist the devil, and he will flee from you." If we will resist the enemy, he must flee.

The issue isn't one of resistance so much as it is one of submission. It's not just that we resist the devil; it's that we submit to God. Our strength comes through our submission. Submit to God, resist the devil. As long as we live in submission to God, the devil has no ground in our lives.

Chapter Ten

Praying for Others

ntercession is basically praying for others. The ministry of intercession is a very high calling. However, unless we understand the difference between being a prayer warrior and being an intercessor, we could get confused. All Christians have an obligation to intercede for others, although some seem to have more of a ministry in intercession than others.

Prayer Warrior

There is a difference between being a prayer warrior and being an intercessor. A prayer warrior is someone who prays specifically from a long list. He prays for many things everyday. First Thessalonians 1:2 gives us a simple illustration of that when it says, "We give thanks to God always for you all, making mention of you in our prayers."

Paul the Apostle traveled considerably. Many people came to him over and over asking for prayer. Apparently Paul's list of people to pray for became quite long because he says, "I make mention of you in my prayers." It's possible that's all he had time for. A prayer warrior will pray for many things every day. They don't necessarily pray until they get an answer. They pray from a list. The prayer warrior is the most common type of pray-er.

Intercessor

The other type of pray-er is the intercessor. The intercessor gives himself to fewer things, but he prays them through. What I mean by "praying through" is that he prays until the burden is lifted from him. "Praying through" is a rather outdated phrase. We don't use it much any more because we live in an instant society. We have everything in an instant. The old definition of praying through is "praying until God gives you a release." The release may come in a short amount of time or it may take a long time, but an intercessor carries the burden until there is a release.

The intercessor can't really develop a long list of things to pray for because of the deep burden he carries for each thing he prays for. He prays for fewer things but he prays them through, whereas the prayer warrior prays from a long list of things every day.

God has designed each of us to be one type of pray-er or the other. One is not more significant than the other. We need people who are lifting all sorts of things (warrior) as well as those who will grab something and not let go (intercessor).

The Supreme Intercessor

Hebrews 7:25 talks about Christ as being the supreme intercessor: "Wherefore he is able also to save them to the uttermost that come unto God by him, seeing he ever liveth to make intercession for them." Christ lives for the purpose of intercession. He gives Himself to praying for others all the time.

Christ is supreme in intercession because of how He identifies with us:

> Forasmuch then as the children are partakers of flesh and blood, he also himself likewise took part of the same; that through death he might destroy him that had the power of death, that is, the devil. . . . For in that he himself hath suffered being tempted, he is able to succour them that are tempted (Heb. 2:14-18).

Christ saw that we were made up of flesh and blood, so he took part of the same. In other words, the Word became flesh. He did this for two reasons. One is that He would defeat the one who has the power of death, that is the devil. Second, being a man and going through temptation, He is able now to come to our aid in the midst of our temptation. He identifies with you and me. He became what you and I are in order to offer us salvation and also to make His praying for us more effective.

We have a problem here, and that is that we can't necessarily become what another man is in order to pray for him. Christ became what we are, but we don't want to become ill just so we can better pray for sick people. We don't want to become a thief just so we can better pray for thieves. Therefore, we must deal more with the spirit of identification than anything else.

The Spirit of Identification

The spirit of identification implies a willingness to do something we don't have to do. Identification is the essence of intercession. It's doing something we don't have to do, as far as our own personal salvation is concerned. We are not more saved by praying for others. If God prompts us to pray for someone and we choose not to, that doesn't mean that we have lost our salvation. It means that our relationship with God is really not very good and that it needs to be changed. If we are going to become effective intercessors, we will need to be willing to give ourselves to something that we don't technically have to.

The spirit of identification describes the heart of Christ. Jesus was in heaven before He became a man. He was at the right hand of the Father. He did not have to come to earth to enhance or establish His relationship with His Father. That was already in place. What He did, He did for you and me. He did something He didn't have to do as far as His position with God was concerned.

Since we don't necessarily want to become what another man is in order to pray for him, we need to operate under this mode of doing something we don't have to do. We can't necessarily identify with all the problems that people have, so what we need to do is feel what God feels for another man. That comes through spending time in His presence. The more time we spend in prayer, the more we feel what God feels, and the more compelled we become to pray for them. We need to operate under the compassion of God. In this way, we'll continue to pray even though we don't necessarily know exactly what the person is going through.

Rees Howells was a man given to intercession. He was once impressed to pray for some children that were starving in India. To do that, he ate one meal a day for a period of time. He said, "If I'm going to pray for starving children, I need to at least understand what it is to be hungry." He went on to say, "I'll deny myself so that I can identify a little more with these kids." He could have eaten his three meals a day and still prayed for those children, but he was willing to do something he didn't have to do just to pray more effectively. That is the spirit of identification.

Agony

We need to consider agony, another aspect of intercession. The intercessor agonizes. In Luke 22:44 we read, "And being in an agony he prayed more earnestly: and his sweat was as it were great drops of blood falling down to the ground." This is the account of Jesus in the Garden of Gethsemane. It teaches us something important about intercession. When we are in agony, we pray more earnestly. Jesus prayed with such fervency and agony that he actually sweat drops of blood. I used to think that Christ could do that because He was God. Then I had a nurse tell me that within each of our sweat glands are blood vessels that can burst under enough pressure. It would take a lot of strain, but under enough stress they could burst and we, too, could sweat drops of blood. Once we understand this, we quickly realize how very little agonizing is really taking place. This helps make Hebrews 12:4 clear to us, "You have not yet resisted to the point of shedding blood in your striving against sin" (NAS). I don't know of anyone that has resisted sin the way Christ did. When it comes to the issue of intercession, our biggest problem is that we lack the kind of compassion Christ had. From the lack of compassion, we do not give ourselves over to these kinds of things. The lack of compassion comes from the lack of time spent in the presence of God.

Two Types of Suffering

There are two types of suffering that we see in the Scriptures. The first one is suffering for Christ. In Acts 16:23 we read, "And when they had laid many stripes upon them, they cast them into prison, charging the jailer to keep them safely." This is an account of someone suffering for Christ. It's suffering for the cause of Christ. There are many people around the world who are suffering even today for the cause of Christ. They fall under the category of being a martyr.

The other type of suffering is suffering with Christ:

> But rejoice, inasmuch as ye are partakers of Christ's sufferings; that, when his glory shall be revealed, ye may be glad also with exceeding joy (1 Pet. 4:13).

There is a difference between suffering for Christ and suffering with Christ. There might be people suffering for Christ who do not suffer with Him at all. The man who is suffering with Christ might find himself in jail for the cause of Christ, but that is not his greatest concern. His greatest concern is that the jailer does not know Jesus. When the jailer brings him his food, his heart breaks over the lostness of the jailer. Such a believer suffers with the things that Christ suffers with.

On the other hand, there could be people in jail who really don't share or fellowship in Christ's sufferings even though they are suffering because they are Christians. It is more common to suffer for Christ than suffer with Christ. To be broken over the lostness of a man means that the things that we are suffering *for* the Lord really don't matter that much. What really grips our heart is the sufferings we share with Christ.

We don't fellowship in the sufferings of Christ until we give ourselves to prayer. In prayer we gain the heart of God. Our hearts have to beat after His heart, but if we don't spend time in His presence, we get away from that and we get strictly into religiosity. We need more than religion. We need the heart of Christ.

Chapter Eleven

The Heart of Intercession

o understand the heart of an intercessor, we must first look into a teaching of Christ concerning disciplining a brother.

Moreover if thy brother shall trespass against thee, go and tell him his fault between thee and him alone: if he shall hear thee, thou hast gained thy brother. But if he will not hear thee, then take with thee one or two more, that in the mouth of two or three witnesses every word may be established. And if he shall neglect to hear them, tell it unto the church: but if he neglect to hear the church, let him be unto thee as a heathen man and a publican. Verily I say unto you, Whatsoever ye shall bind on earth shall be bound in heaven: and whatsoever ye shall loose on earth shall be loosed in heaven. Again I say unto you, That if two of you shall agree

on earth as touching any thing that they
shall ask, it shall be done for them of
my Father which is in heaven. For
where two or three are gathered together in my name, there am I in the
midst of them (Matt. 18:15-20).

Two or Three

In verse 16 we are told to take two or three witnesses with us to discipline a brother. The "two or
three" witnesses in verse 16 are the same "two or
three" witnesses mentioned in verse 20 where it says,
"For where two or three are gathered together in my
name, there am I in the midst of them." This must be
one of the most misapplied verses in the Bible. Ministers will typically use this verse to make themselves
feel better about small meetings. If very few people
show up for a meeting, the pastor will refer to verse
20 and say, "Well, the Bible tells us that if two or
three are gathered together in His name, He is there
with them." It's almost as if Jesus wasn't enough.
It's true that Jesus is present when we gather together
in His name, but to say that it takes two or three believers to gather before He shows up is terrible theol-
ogy. Christ abides not only with *groups* of believers,
for each believer has an ever-abiding presence of the
Holy Spirit in his heart. Any believer can go into the
prayer closet all by himself and find that Christ is
there with him. Verse 20 is referring to the two or
three witnesses that have gone along to bring disci-

pline to a brother. What Christ was getting at was the unity of the witnesses. He was saying that wherever two or three have agreed upon something in His name, He would be with them in their decision. That is why verse 18 says, "Whatsoever ye shall bind on earth shall be bound in heaven: and whatsoever ye shall loose on earth shall be loosed in heaven." Christ was simply telling them that He would honor whatever decisions they had come to because of the unity of their hearts.

Symphony

To understand unity, we need to look at a word in Matthew 18:19: "Again I say unto you, That if two of you shall agree on earth as touching any thing that they shall ask, it shall be done for them of my Father which is in heaven." The word "agree" is the Greek word *sumphoneo*. *Sumphoneo* is the word that we get our word "symphony" from. The root of this word is the word "phone." "Phone" has do with our voice. "Telephone" is one example of this word. When you add the prefix and the suffix to the base of this word, it means the harmonizing of voices. When our voices harmonize in prayer, we make a symphony unto the Lord. R.A. Torrey, the great 19th century Bible teacher, once said, "We are agreeing to pray together, but we are not really agreeing in prayer for each other." If we are going to actually agree in prayer with another person, our heart must share the burden of the one we are praying for.

Our hearts are what actually pray. When we pray, God hears the cry or the burden of our heart. We speak out of the abundance of our hearts. Prayer is simply a verbal expression of that which we feel in our hearts. If a brother or sister in Christ asks us to agree in prayer over a burdensome issue, we need to consider our response carefully. If we determine we are going to agree with that person in prayer, then it will require much more than simply taking their hands and praying over the issue for a few seconds.

Suppose someone comes to us with a very heavy burden. His heart is broken over a certain issue in his life. He asks us if we will agree with him in prayer, and we agree to do so. During our prayer time together, if we don't share his burden, our prayer will have an empty sound to it. If their heart is groaning out their deep feelings while we have a very light-hearted, cheerleading attitude, there has been no symphony. I have watched many people pray cheerleading prayers and then claim that since they prayed together, God must now answer. God is not obligated to answer until we meet His conditions. If one's heart makes a certain sound, one full of compassion, but his heart contains no compassion at all, we have not met qualifications for "agreeing," so we cannot claim Matthew 18:19 at all.

First Corinthians 13:1 says that if we do not have love, we are like sounding brass or tinkling cymbals. If we do not share in our brother's burden, we lack love. Without love, our prayer sounds tinny. It lacks depth, it lacks feeling, it does not reflect the heart of Christ at all. It cannot harmonize with someone else's burden at all. We can easily agree to pray with others, but to agree in prayer with them takes much more than simply the act of two people praying together over the same issue.

God Heals

Several years ago I was impressed to agree in prayer with a woman who was suffering from rheumatoid arthritis. This was a young woman in her twenties who was about to be confined to a wheelchair because of the severity of her pain. God gave me this impression to pray for her while my wife and I were visiting with them. I did not struggle with the idea of agreeing in prayer for her, so I began to move toward her with the idea of praying for her right there. As I began to move God said, "Don't pray now." This was very confusing to me because I never felt it would ever be wrong to pray. Yet at this time, God was impressing me to simply pray about praying for her. So I determined to include her in my prayers each time I prayed for the next few days.

After a few days of praying for her, I felt a release from the Lord to call her and to tell her that I was going to agree in prayer with her concerning her illness. I made the phone call, she thanked me, and that was about all that happened. However, about a week later, I began to get very burdened for her. The Lord began to wake me up in the middle of the night to pray for her. I would be awakened out of a sound sleep with a tremendous burden for her. This burden lasted three hours each time. It had such a grip on my heart that I simply could not let go of it. Each night, in the middle of the night, I would pray for three hours for her. I knew in my heart that if I did not pray, something would not happen which would happen if I prayed.

After about a week, the burden lifted. I was no longer being awakened each night, and I simply knew that God had done something. About a week after the burden lifted, she went to see her doctor. He told her that for the first time in her medical history, her situation was reversing itself. She was getting better. It has now been well over a decade, and she never has used a wheelchair, and she works everyday. God healed her.

God taught me something through that whole experience. Agreeing in prayer with someone is not a flippant thing. It's not something that we simply decide to do. When I first felt God impress me to pray for her, I thought I would simply get up and pray for her for a few seconds, and that would be that. I would have fulfilled my obligation to God. However, God was looking for someone to share her burden. Therefore, He needed to prepare me for this. That is why He said, "Don't pray now." As I was praying about agreeing in prayer for her, God was preparing my heart for something about which I had no knowledge at all. As God began to awaken me each night with a burden to pray, my heart would ache for her. As I was in the midst of praying for her, at one point, I believe my burden matched hers. At that point, I believe God said in essence, "There's the symphony, there's the answer!"

It's not that we are in some type of contest, and once we have reached a certain level, God answers our prayers. It's that God is looking for those who will reflect His heart. When our burden matches someone else's burden, then our heart is emulating His heart. When we hurt, God hurts. When we cry, God cries. God wants others to know that He cares. The only way for Him to reveal that to others is through those who carry His Spirit. God wants to reveal himself to others through His children, but they must reflect His heart in order to do that.

Make Me Miserable

The heart of intercession can be summed up in another true incident. Many years ago, a man decided to attend a prayer meeting. In this particular meeting, the men prayed on one side of the room, and the women prayed on the other side of the room. A bed sheet was hung down the center of the room to separate them. As the man knelt at a chair to pray, he happened to be right next to the sheet, and he could hear a woman who was on the other side of the sheet praying. He could hear that her heart was really broken, and she was praying for someone who was spiritually lost. He assumed that it was a lost relative, or child. She was praying a very desperate prayer.

She was saying, "Lord do what ever you have to do to save him. Don't let him eat until he makes you his Lord. Don't let him sleep until he makes you his Lord. Make him miserable until he gives his heart to you."

The man was so moved with the burden of her heart that he decided that he would pray for the same person. As he began to pray, he was totally surprised at what came out of his mouth. He said, "Lord, don't let *me* eat until he makes you his Lord. Don't let *me* sleep until he makes you his Lord. Make *me* miserable until he gives his heart to you."

The heart of the intercessor takes on another person's burden. It's actually allowing another person's problem to control our lives. We don't like to lose control, but the whole idea of submission is that we give up control. Our sinful nature still controls Christ. So why shouldn't the problems of others control us? Christ still spends all of His time in intercession. He still lives influenced by the sinfulness of men. It is actually ungodly to refuse to give ourselves in praying for others. To refuse to pray for others is similar to saying, "I'm in control of my life. I'll do what I want, and other people's needs don't really affect me." That attitude is quite contrary to who Christ is. Christ set an example for us by allowing other people's needs to determine His lifestyle.

Chapter Twelve

How to Develop Your Prayer Life

his chapter was placed toward the end of the book for a reason. It contains the practical aspects of developing your prayer life. It is probably the most important chapter in the whole book, because without it we could end up with a desire to pray but never really develop into people that seek God. Undoubtedly some of you recognize that your lack of prayer is from the lack of spiritual discipline in your life. Subsequently, you scanned the table of contents of this book and found this chapter titled "How to Develop Your Prayer Life." You quickly moved to this chapter thinking this is the shortcut to the prayer life. Wrong! Go back and read the rest of the book before you read this chapter, or you will miss the message.

Central Time of Prayer

When it comes to developing our prayer life, there are several things that must be understood. When talking about our prayer time, I am not talking about the sum total of our prayer life. I am referring to when we have our central time of prayer daily. It is very important for us to have a central time of prayer each day. From that time of prayer, we may have all sorts of other times and types of prayer in our lives. We may find ourselves praying while in the car, shooting little "arrow-prayers" to the Lord. We may find ourselves stopping in the middle of the day for a short time of prayer over an urgent need of which we have just been made aware. However, those types of prayers do not really feed us the way our central time of prayer does.

When it comes to discussing the development of our prayer life, we are not focusing on these "other" times of prayer. We are focusing specifically on the central time of prayer.

Habit

When it comes to discussing the habit of prayer, we may initially have some negative reaction to that. There are some connotations to the word "habit" that are not necessarily good. We often equate habits with bad habits. However, a habit is not inherently evil. Certainly there are bad habits, but there are also good habits. Prayer would fall on the side of a good habit. Brushing your teeth is a good habit, but good habits are not noticed as much as bad habits are. Good habits are often done without even thinking. They are the type of things we have done so often that they are instinctive. A habit is defined as something we have repeated so often that it has become involuntary. It would be great if each of us could get to this place in our prayer lives.

Often I will ask people if they believe it's easy to fall out of their prayer life. Many times they say, "Yes." I disagree with that. We don't just fall out of any habit. There are two ways that we come out of habits. One is that God delivers us. God can deliver us miraculously from habits. The other way is that we work our way out of a habit the same way we worked our way into a habit. We must discipline ourselves out of a habit. Since those are the two ways we get out of habits, we can rest assured of one thing. When it comes to the habit of prayer, God won't deliver us from it. I have yet to meet a man who said God delivered him from his prayer life. Wouldn't it be interesting to find someone who said, "I had a great prayer life going, and then one day God delivered me from it." It just doesn't work that way. God does not set us free from things that help us draw closer to Him. We don't just fall out of any habit. We would have to deliberately keep refusing the prodding of the Holy Spirit until that habit dies. When a person says that it's an easy habit to fall out of, what they are really saying is that they have never really developed a deep prayer life.

Legalism

People also tend to believe a habit of prayer could become legalistic. Legalism is trying to find favor with God through our actions. The Pharisees often prayed with that particular motive. They thought God would hear them if they prayed a lot. I don't believe it would be good for anybody to get in bondage to prayer. There is a significant difference between legalism and holiness, though outwardly they often are difficult to distinguish. The attitude of our heart is frequently the only difference. If we are praying because we want to be with God, then we are separating ourselves from the world for the right reasons, which results in holiness. If we are praying because we think we should, to keep in favor with God, we miss the greater purpose and become nothing more than a legalist.

If we compare this to a man courting a woman, we can understand better. A man will look for ways to be with her. When I was courting my soon-to-be wife, I never felt like I was spending too much time with her. I never thought that because I was with her yesterday, I shouldn't be with her today for fear of becoming entangled in bondage. I wasn't in bondage. I was in love, and when you're in love, you can't get too much of a good thing. When we pray because we want God, even though we may be making ourselves pray, it's not legalistic at all. I used to arrange my schedule to court my wife. I made myself do it, but it was still not bondage, it was love. Many days I will find that prior to spending time with the Lord, I feel something inside reminding me that I haven't yet prayed. It's the same gnawing any person feels when they have a habit. It is a constant reminder to do something. It's not legalism, it's love.

The Prayer Habit Developed

It would be nice to be at the place where prayer draws us. However, to get to that place takes deliberate action. If the habit of prayer was a simple thing to develop, then we would all be better pray-ers than we are. Paul said, "The things I don't want to do, I'm doing and the things I want to do, I'm not doing" (Rom. 7:15, paraphrased). Galatians 5:17 describes the battle we all face. "For the flesh lusteth against the Spirit, and the Spirit against the flesh: and these are contrary the one to the other: so that ye cannot do the things that ye would." Prayer is a difficult thing for our flesh. In order to bring our flesh under, and to give the spirit control, we need to do some things first.

Establish a Time Goal

We must establish a time goal. A time goal is necessary to determine the minimum amount of time that we want to spend in prayer. The goal should never be used to determine the maximum amount of time we will spend in prayer, but rather the minimum. In using a time goal we are telling ourselves how little time we will pray. It's a discipline for the pray-er. We are not to tell the Lord how much time we will pray, we are simply telling ourselves how little time we will pray. If we pray beyond our goal, that's not a problem. The goal is a discipline for us to help us develop the habit.

> And he cometh unto the disciples,
> and findeth them asleep, and saith unto
> Peter, What, could ye not watch with
> me one hour? (Matt. 26:40).

The "hour" is the only reference to time and prayer in the Word. There is one exception to that where the Word refers to people praying all night long. It would be quite unreasonable to expect anybody to pray all night long every night, but we could easily pray one hour each day. This is not a doctrine. This is merely a suggestion based on Scripture and personal testimony. The Bible does not teach that we must pray an hour a day. It's just that the hour of prayer is the only real reference we have from the Scriptures. Obviously, we can pray less than an hour a day, also. God will personalize our prayer lives and bring us into exactly what He wants for us.

Without a goal, we have no way to measure our progress or measure our success. If we simply go to prayer without any goal, we will pray until we feel like we are done. We may not have spent much time at it at all, yet we will feel as though we are finished because we had no goal that we were trying to reach. Suppose we set a goal, and then go to prayer. After we feel we have said it all, we may look at our watch and realize we haven't even come close to our goal.

However, that's not a problem. We can simply go back to prayer. It is not a difficult thing to make ourselves pray. If we would spend 5 minutes praying for every person we know who needs prayer, it would take us 30 minutes to pray for just 6 people. Praying for 12 people will take us an hour. We don't run out of things to pray for. We run out of a structure in which to work, and the time goal is part of that structure.

Establish a Set Time

Now we must consider establishing a set time for prayer. We do not need to try to pray at exactly the same time every day. However, every day we need to determine when we are going to pray. If we don't determine when we will pray, we will find that it's very easy to skip prayer. How does setting a time to pray fit in with being led? "Shouldn't we pray when the Spirit leads us?" Certainly! We should pray every time the Spirit leads us. However, leading ourselves to prayer is no less spiritual. In Luke 18:1 we read: "And he spake a parable unto them to this end, that men ought always to pray, and not to faint." The word "ought" means an act of the will. Jesus was teaching us that men need to lead themselves to prayer, that prayer is an act of the will. If you say to the Lord, "I've got time today at 3:00 p.m. I'm going to pray then." God will probably say, "Good, it will be good to hear from you finally." God will be pleased whenever you decide to pray. However, if we have determined to pray at a certain time of the day and suddenly we feel led to pray sooner, we need to obey the Spirit. It would not be right to say, "I'm sorry God, but I don't pray until 3:00 p.m." That could be a problem. The fact that we have determined to pray at a certain time does not mean that we cannot pray whenever the Spirit leads us.

We can pray anytime God wants us to pray, but we are dealing with the development of the prayer habit. To develop the habit, we need to deliberately establish a prayer time. Once prayer has its grips on us, it will motivate us. We won't need to be as deliberate. It will be more natural. However, at first, it's very deliberate.

Praying Without Ceasing

Some may ask: "How does praying without ceasing fit into all of this?" Praying without ceasing is the development of a mindset that continually focuses on God. It's similar to carrying on a continual conversation with God. We may find ourselves talking to God while we are on our jobs. Some housewives may find themselves praying while they are cleaning their homes. I believe these are all positive things, up to a point. We must remember that we are seeking to develop a relationship with God. Relationships require intimacy. Intimacy demands privacy. How healthy would a man's relationship with his wife be if the only time he spoke to her was while he was working on his car? Some people try to justify their lack of setting a specific time of prayer aside by praying during their work. Though there is nothing wrong with praying all day, if there is no element of private prayer in their life, their intimacy with God is not very deep. Private prayer is what fuels praying without ceasing. If you really want to spend your day focusing in on God, then have a time of intimacy with Him early in your day. The things that occupy our minds the most are intimacies. It's from giving yourself to God in prayer that you find you can't get your mind off of Him.

A Priority of Prayer

In Matthew 21:13 we read: "It is written, My house shall be called the house of prayer; but ye have made it a den of thieves." In this statement, Christ was making prayer pre-eminent. That which should stand out above all things, in the house of God, should be prayer. Today, the believer is the house of God. Prayer is to have first place in our lives, otherwise we will rob God. If prayer is not pre-eminent, other things will always get in our way to keep us from praying. If we ever want to remember all of the things that we should be doing, just decide to spend some time in prayer. As soon as we begin to pray, our mind is cluttered with all of the things that we think we should be getting done. If we don't have a priority, then all of those things will always keep us from praying.

And they entered into a covenant
to seek the Lord God of their fathers

with all their heart and with all their
soul (2 Chron. 15:12).

Entering into a covenant requires priority. In this
case, seeking God, was the priority. They wanted to
be close to God, so they determined that they would
seek God with all their heart and with all their soul.
The heart and soul make up the essence of man. To
have a priority of seeking God, we must make a covenant which puts God first in our lives. Seeking God
must take priority over sleeping, comfort, and con-
venience. Without this type of commitment, we will
never develop a life of prayer. Prayer will simply remain the thing we do when we want something from
God. Prayer will lack intimacy in our lives.

Chapter Thirteen

The Hour of Prayer

he Lord's Prayer offers us a simple break-down of how to spend time in prayer. It contains five areas of focus. In each area, I will suggest an adequate amount of time to be spent in prayer. These amounts of time will add up to one hour. Obviously we are free to spend as much time as we choose in each area. This is simply given as a help for those who feel they need assistance in spending time in prayer. We will look into each portion as recorded in Matthew 6.

1. Worship.

In verse 9 we read, "After this manner therefore pray ye: Our Father which art in heaven, Hallowed be thy name." Jesus begins this prayer by worshiping the name of His Father. This is meant to be a time of proclaiming your adoration to the Lord. Tell Him how much you want Him or need Him or love Him. Worship Him!

It's important to begin our prayer time in worship. It clears our minds, and gets us thinking about God. Worship helps us to make the transition from the flesh to the spirit. Many times prayer begins in the flesh. Often we are praying out of obedience more than anything else. Worship changes all of that and brings us into God's presence. It sets the tone for the rest of the prayer time. Spend a minimum of **ten minutes** worshipping the Lord.

2. Intercession.

Matthew 6:10 says, "Thy kingdom come. Thy will be done in earth, as it is in heaven." Praying for the Kingdom to come is the same as praying for Christ to dwell in the hearts of men. There is no kingdom of God outside of Christ dwelling in a man. Christ said in Luke 17:21, "Neither shall they say, Lo here! or, lo there! for, behold, the kingdom of God is within you." When we pray, "your kingdom come," we are praying for the souls of men. We are praying for Jesus to occupy men's hearts. This should take up the largest portion of our prayer time. It would not be very difficult to spend 30 minutes simply praying for others. If we pray 5 minutes for each person that God has put on our heart, 6 people will take 30 minutes at 5 minutes each. It is really a simple thing to spend time in intercession because there are so many people that need help. Determine to pray for at least **thirty minutes** in intercession everyday.

3. Petition.

Matthew 6:11 says, "Give us this day our daily bread." Petition is that of praying for our own needs. This comes most naturally to us. However, that there is a subtle trick the enemy likes to play on us we need to be aware. If we spend all of our time praying for ourselves, we burn out and fail to pray for others. It is very easy for our own needs to occupy our thoughts. However, God is trying to teach us to not be so self-centered. The best way to get our own prayers answered is to pray for others. When we concern ourselves with the needs of others, God concerns himself with our needs.

The greatest need all of us have is for more of Christ. Many times our time of petition should simply be that of praying to be filled with Christ and His Spirit. Intimacy with Christ is the answer to every situation we face. Spend a minimum of **five minutes** in petition.

4. Confession.

Matthew 6:12-13 reads, "And forgive us our debts, as we forgive our debtors. And lead us not into temptation, but deliver us from evil." In these verses, we are expressing the hidden parts of our heart. David prayed, "Behold, thou desirest truth in the inward parts: and in the hidden part thou shalt make me to know wisdom" (Ps. 51:6). He knew the importance of a clean heart. This is a very important facet of prayer. We need the daily habit of saying, "God, here is my heart. Show me the things in my heart that are not pleasing to you." We should ask God to show us if there are wrong attitudes, wrong motives, or even wrong priorities in our lives. Psalms 139:23-24 are excellent verses for this. "Search me, O God, and know my heart: try me, and know my thoughts, and see if there be any wicked way in me, and lead me in the way everlasting." When God reveals things to you that are displeasing to Him, simply confess them. Ask Him to forgive you. The only reason He shows us these things is to reconcile himself to us. God does not reveal these things out of anger, but rather, out of compassion. Spend a minimum of **five minutes** in this section.

5. Worship.

We begin with worship and end with worship. The last part of Matthew 6:13 says, "For thine is the kingdom, and the power, and the glory, for ever. Amen." God is worthy of our worship. The most appropriate way to end your time with Him is by worshiping Him once more. Spend another **ten minutes** worshiping God.

Conclusion

Prayer is a choice. God does not force us to pray. It is an act of our will. Once we choose to be with God and develop a desire to be with Him, it changes our lives. It causes us to see what He sees. It causes us to hear what He hears. It causes us to think what He thinks. It develops His heart in us. It will become the greatest blessing in your life. May God bless you in this adventure into Him!

John Hagee

Pearls.   S-818
from The Pen

PO BX 1400
San Antonio, TX
78295